Old Cotswold Photographs

by

D. J. Viner, B.A., A.M.A.

Curator of the Corinium Museum,
Cirencester

Front cover: The High Street, *Chipping Campden*, about 1890

First edition July 1977
Second impression May 1989

Published by Hendon Publishing Co. Ltd., Hendon Mill, Nelson, Lancashire

Printed by Netherwood Dalton & Co. Ltd., Huddersfield

INDEX

THE Cotswolds is a recognisable geographical area, a characteristically upland region mainly in Gloucestershire extending significantly into Oxfordshire, Warwickshire and the new County of Avon. It has always been identifiable to both residents and visitors and its physical attraction as an area in which to live has ensured no little interest in its history and topography. The general tone of the resultant writing on the Cotswolds has been sympathetic even laudatory, although there have been exceptions; William Cobbett found the shallow soils and the dry-stone walls unsatisfying in 1826. The area was, he exclaimed, 'a sort of country having less to please the eye than any other that I have ever seen'.

Today the Cotswold region is under great pressure from many sources. The desirability of living in the countryside but with good access to motorways and hence to Birmingham, Bristol and London threaten a kind of dormitory status, and this together with the expanding 'holiday home industry' has drastically changed the village way of life out of all recognition.

At the same time, visitors in their thousands come to see village life at close quarters, and make demands upon it which can only adequately be satisfied by threatening the very attraction itself. It seems appropriate to pause in the midst of these modern pressures and to recall a different age, over fifty years ago, when the pace of country life was determined by factors altogether different from those of today.

This album does not seek to be a history of the period nor a comprehensive survey of the area, but it is intended to catch a glimpse of Cotswold life and thus some appreciation of the social history of a predominantly rural community.

There is no definite time-limit – several of the photographs included here post-date the second world war, but their subject matter is far older; the travelling shop, for example, belongs to its period just as much as the carrier's cart of an earlier generation.

From the choice of photographs available, a selection has been made to present most areas of the Cotswolds, with a gravitation perhaps towards the central axis along the Fosse Way. This is quite arbitrary although it is hoped that further opportunities may allow for a more extensive coverage.

Within the scope of this volume, it would be inappropriate to attempt a history or topography of the Cotswolds, indeed far better to refer to the works of those writers more experienced in such matters. The literature on the Cotswolds is extensive and the area still ranks as one of those regions which continue to attract topographical studies at regular intervals. Such books are often worth studying in their own right for the evolution of the approach to 'life in the country' and indeed the Cotswold pedigree is a good one.

In 1898 J. Arthur Gibbs published *A Cotswold Village,* a series of observations on "country life and pursuits in Gloucestershire" and this study has become justifiably famous; it has recently been republished as *Cotswold Countryman* (1967). The village in question is Ablington near Bibury and much of the material is derived from the neighbouring wolds and the river valley of the Coln.

The study of a rural community through the changing seasons of the year was an equally effective medium for two writers in the thirties: C. Henry Warren's *A Cotswold Year* (1936) on the north-west Cotswolds and, also in the north, the renowned country writer H. J. Massingham in *Wold Without End* (1932). Two of Massingham's many other works deserve attention: *Cotswold Country* (1937) covers in fact a much wider area than its title suggests, from Dorset to Lincolnshire, whilst *Country Relics* (1939) examines the crafts of the countryside through the tools and implements in use, many from local sources.

Of the early post-war studies, mention should be made of Freda Derrick's *Cotswold Stone* (1948) and the writing of Edith Brill. A major contribution was made by Prof. H. P. R. Finberg in his *Gloucestershire* (1955) in the Making of the English Landscape series and this volume was republished in 1975.

Of recent work, five volumes merit the attention of all interested students: David Verey's *Gloucestershire* in the Buildings of England series, volume one on the Cotswolds (1970) and his subsequent *Cotswold Churches* (1976), Edith Brill's wide-ranging *Life and Tradition on the Cotswolds* (1973) and in the same year *The Cotswolds: A New Study* edited by Charles & Alice Mary Hadfield; the most recent survey is by Brian Smith, *The Cotswolds* (1976).

Such volumes provide the substance to the way of life glimpsed in these pages, beyond which one need only recommend the childhood memories of Laurie Lee at Slad near Stroud in *Cider With Rosie* (1959) and Fred Archer of Ashton under Hill on the Cotswold outlier at Bredon Hill.

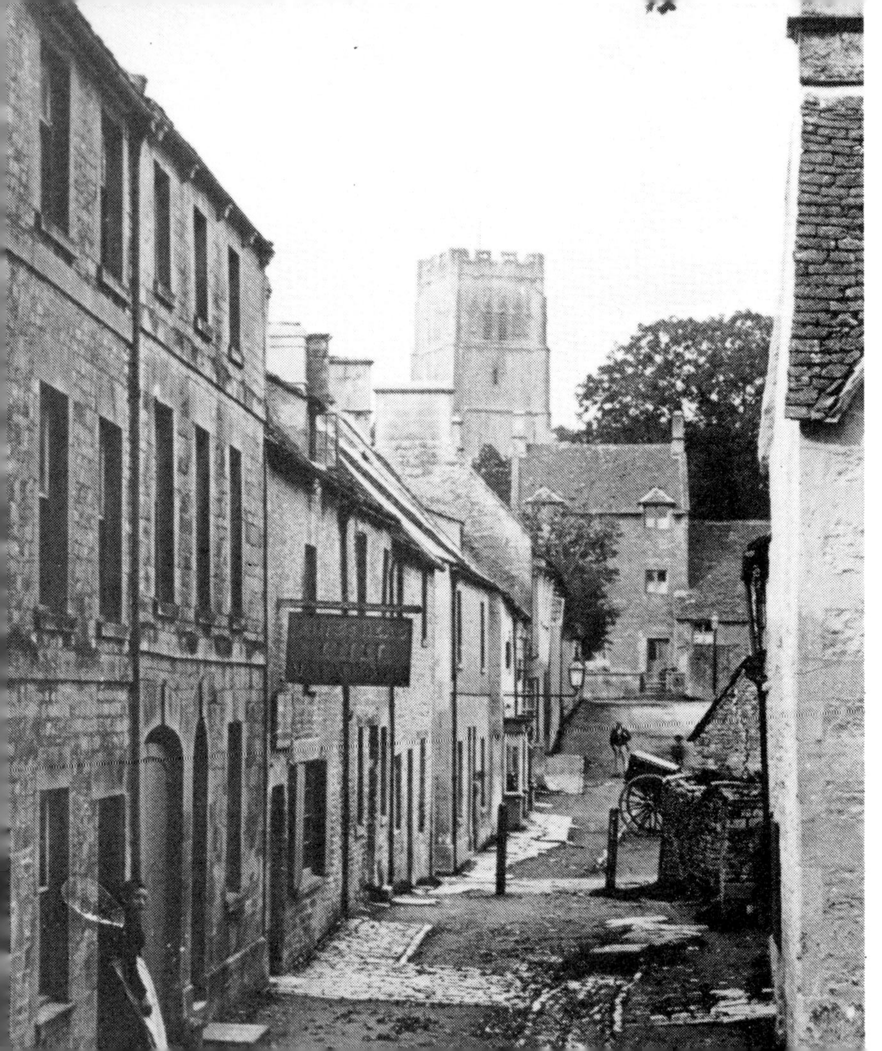

THE TOWNS

The several Cotswold towns are almost invariably characterised by their major reason for existence as market centres. The market place, usually close by the church, dominated the structure of the town and this is true of Lechlade (front cover) which was a market town by the 13th century. Weekly markets were held (no. 15) together with occasional larger fairs.

No. 1 The streets of the town clustered around the market place. In this view of *Northleach* (left) the narrow roadway leads past the Kings Head Inn to the market place beyond, hidden behind a typically Cotswold double-gabled cottage on the right. Little more than a village, Northleach was a major centre for the wool trade in medieval England – hence the impressive nature of the church which dominates the scene as visual evidence of the wealth and piety of the local wool merchants.

By c. 1900 when this photograph was taken Northleach remained in self-contained isolation despite its position close to the junction of two major highways of Gloucestershire. It could boast most of the tradesmen and craftsmen required to sustain life in the centre of an agricultural community.

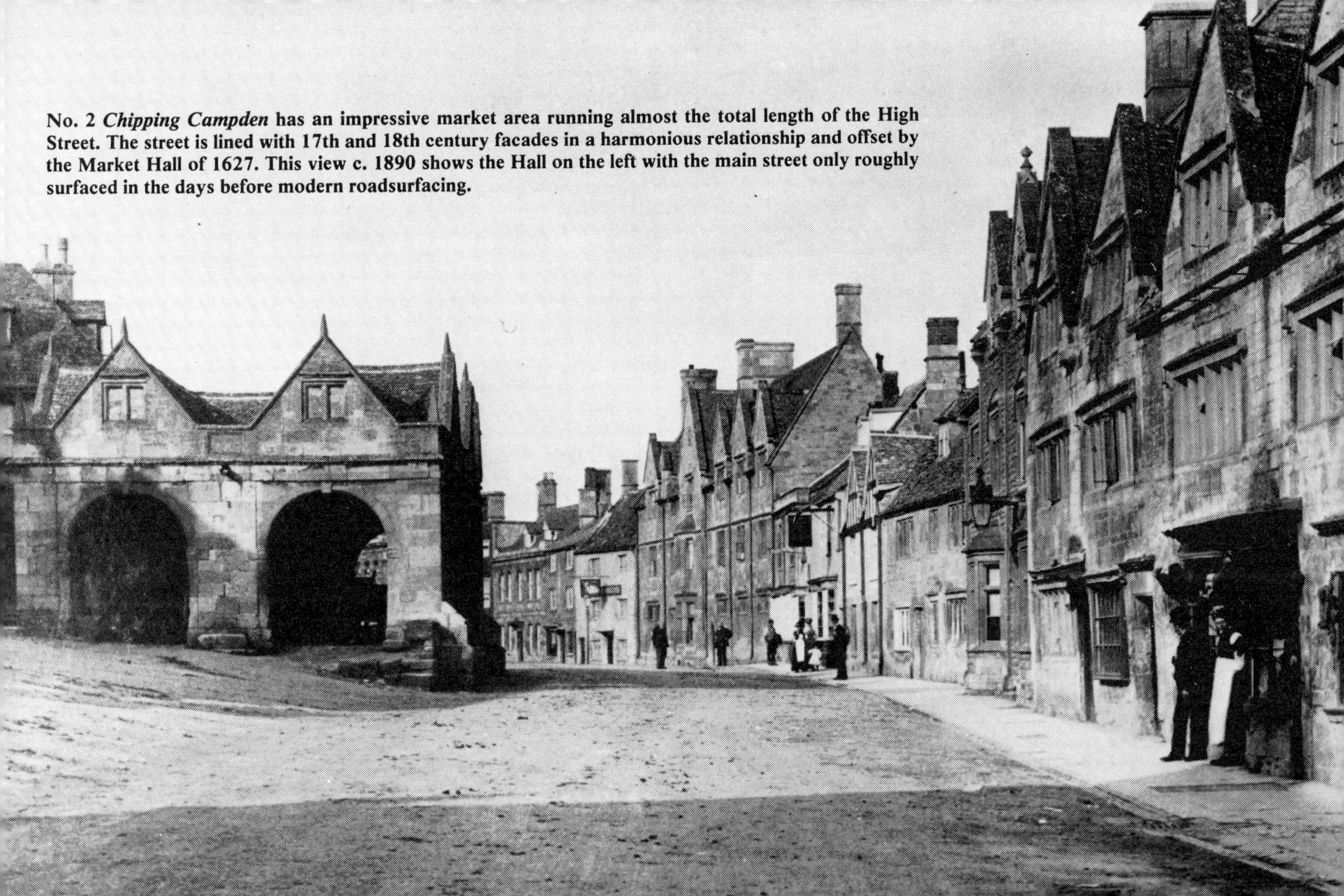

No. 2 *Chipping Campden* has an impressive market area running almost the total length of the High Street. The street is lined with 17th and 18th century facades in a harmonious relationship and offset by the Market Hall of 1627. This view c. 1890 shows the Hall on the left with the main street only roughly surfaced in the days before modern roadsurfacing.

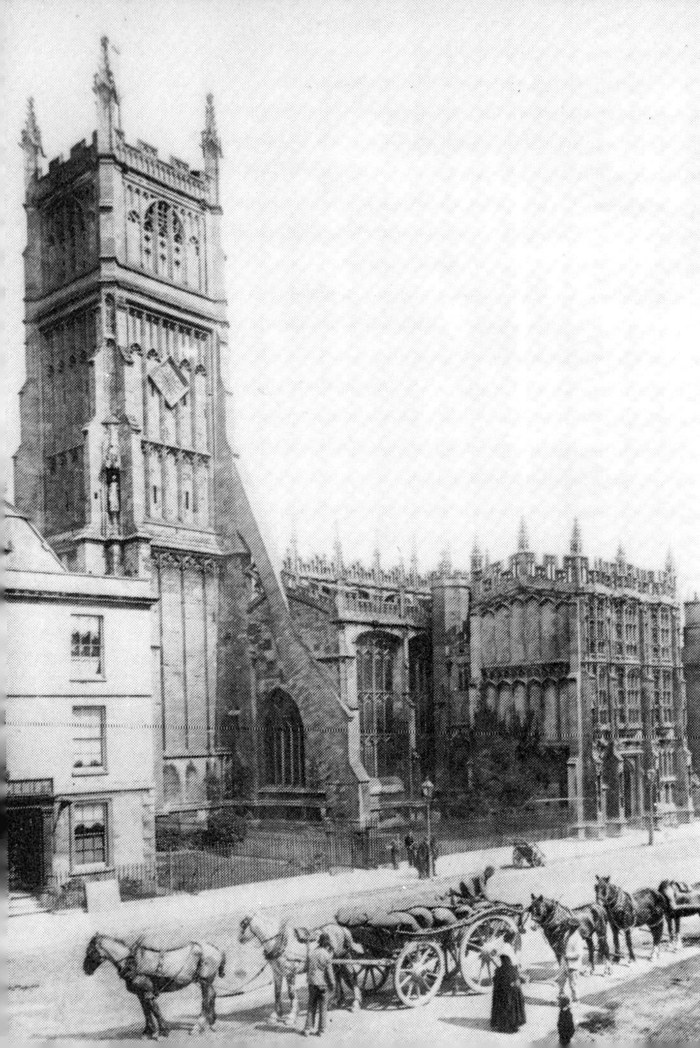

No. 3 *Cirencester's* large market place has been a focal point for commercial life in the south Cotswolds since the Domesday Book recorded that a new market had been set up in the 11th century. Again the 'wealth of wool' is evident here – the parish church of St. John Baptist was rebuilt to almost its present condition in the 15th and 16th centuries.

Until 1830 two rows of houses stood in the market place each distinguished by the trade carried on there: Shoe Lane, Butter Row, and Botcher Row. These were cleared by 1830 and the buildings clustering around the northern side of the church demolished c. 1912.

This postcard view dates from the turn of the century. Note the almost total lack of activity other than that focussed upon the two waggon teams in the foreground.

No. 4 (right) *Stow on the Wold* between the wars. Stow's large market place is now a focal point for summer visitors and the grass around the tree is much reduced for car parking. The stocks remain albeit restored, although the nationally famous sheep and horse fairs have now moved out from the centre of the town. Stow fair-day brought buyers and sellers from miles around and up to 20,000 sheep were said to have been sold at each fair.

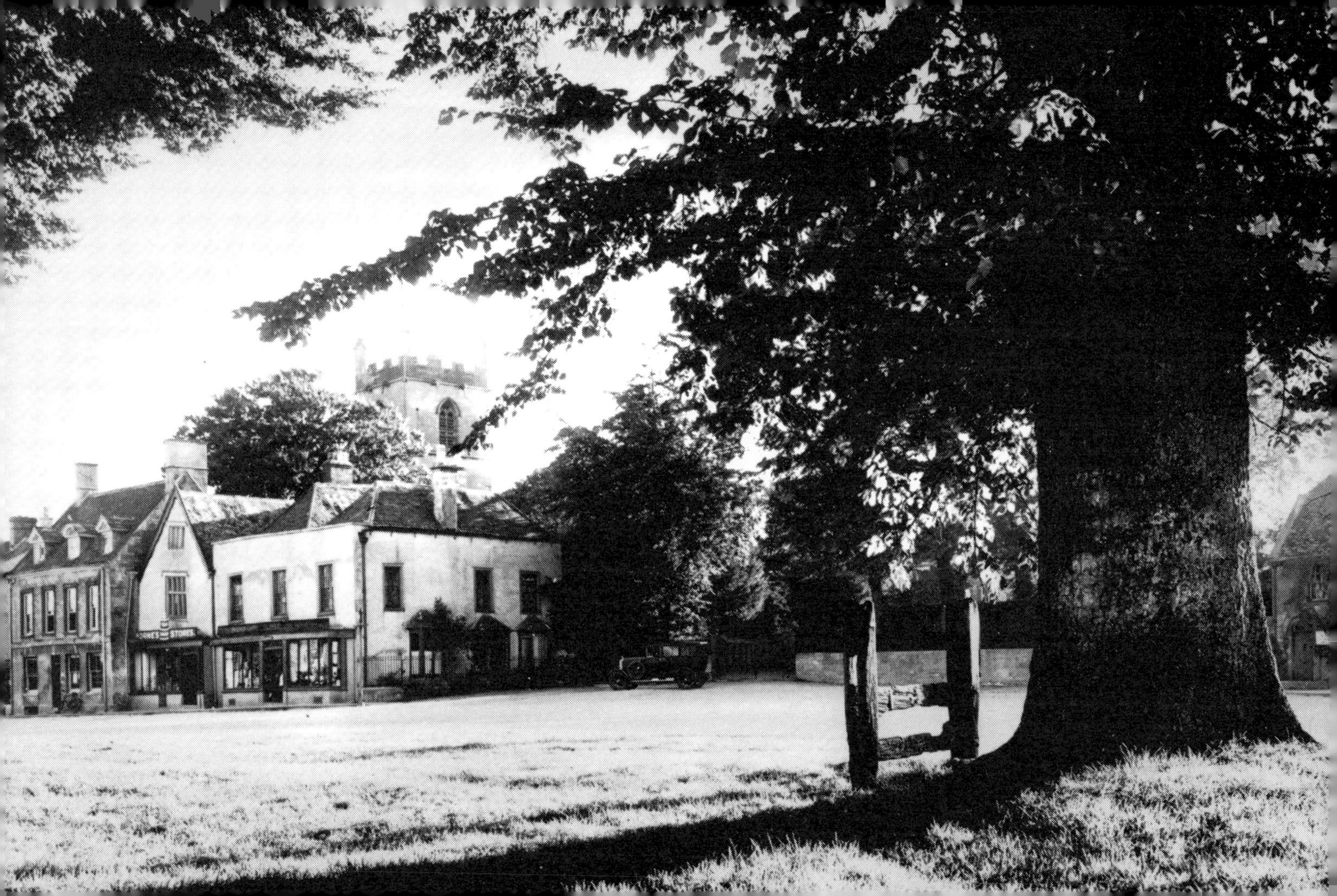

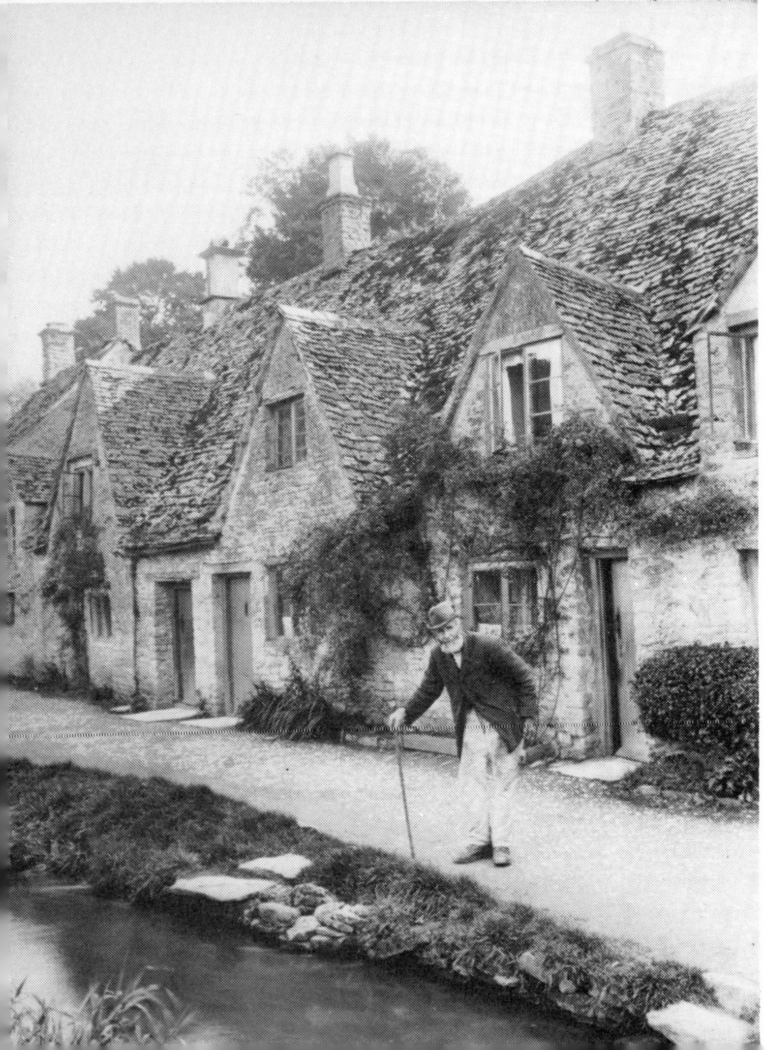

THE VILLAGES

No. 5 Village life as it is often fondly remembered before the first world war: a period of continuity and little change. This is perhaps the classic view – a cottager outside his home in retirement from many years' exacting toil. Certainly, village life had a steady rhythm barely broken and hardly influenced by the outside world. But this 'quaintness' makes no allowances for the real struggle hidden behind, the extremely long hours of work and the constant risk of illness together with the nagging fear that advancing years might not necessarily lead to a comfortable and secure retirement.

Not all villages enjoyed this man's comfort in a row of cottages at *Bibury* now world famous. Arlington Row is the property of the National Trust and recent improvements suggest that the cottages originally formed a barn and were probably used for storing wool.

No. 6 (right) *Bibury* clusters alongside the river Coln which is today a major attraction for visitors. This view shows Arlington Mill which when it was built in the 17th century was used as both a cloth and a corn mill. Most Cotswold villages standing on streams or in river valleys boasted a corn mill and several survive as restorations – Arlington Mill is now an attractive country museum. The external stone buttresses date from the 19th century.

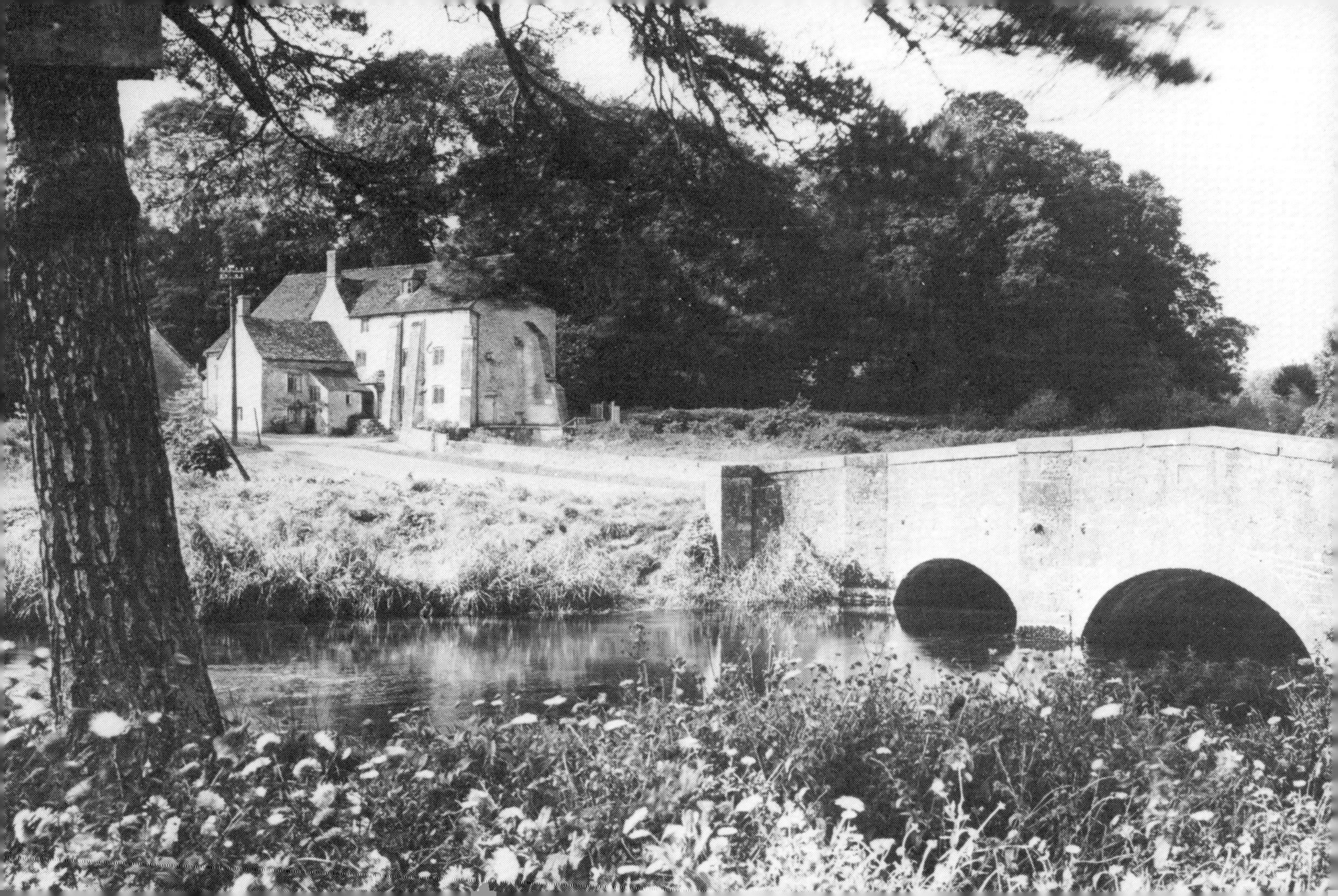

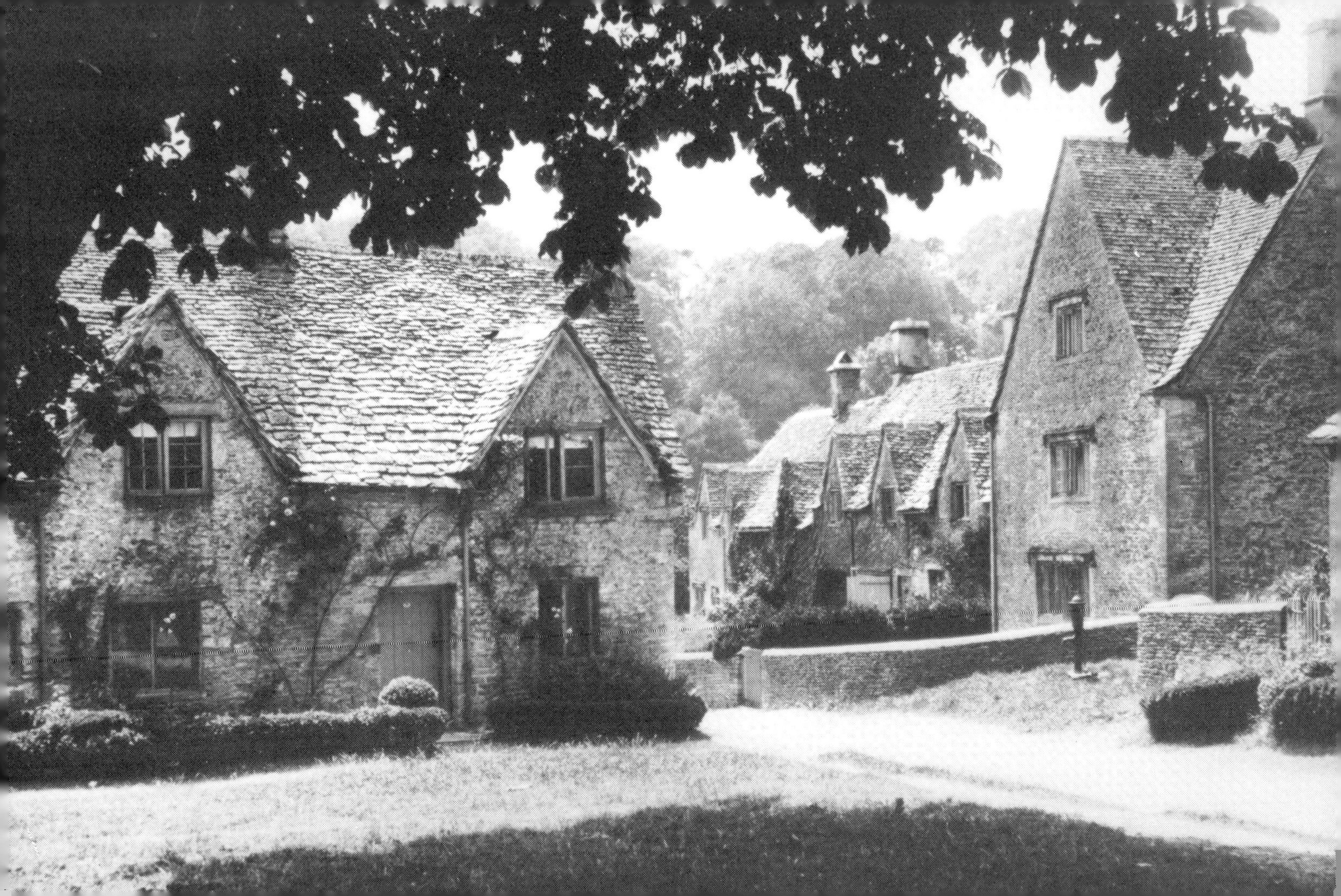

No. 7 The square at *Bibury* – the centre of the village. Note the uniformity of building materials, Cotswold stone for both walls and roofs. The distinctive high-pitched roof is seen here as perhaps the most typical Cotswold feature of the scene. Most of the buildings are 17th century in date and since of course much restored. Current popularity is perhaps greater than ever before and there is a thriving market in 'modernised cottages'.

No. 8 (right) Besides the church the other dominant feature of the village was the manor house; *Bibury* with its associated hamlets has several. This is Bibury Court, a fine mansion alongside the Coln with its date 1633 inscribed over the porch. At the time of this photograph c. 1901 it formed part of a country-wide society of wealth and privilege; today it is a country hotel.

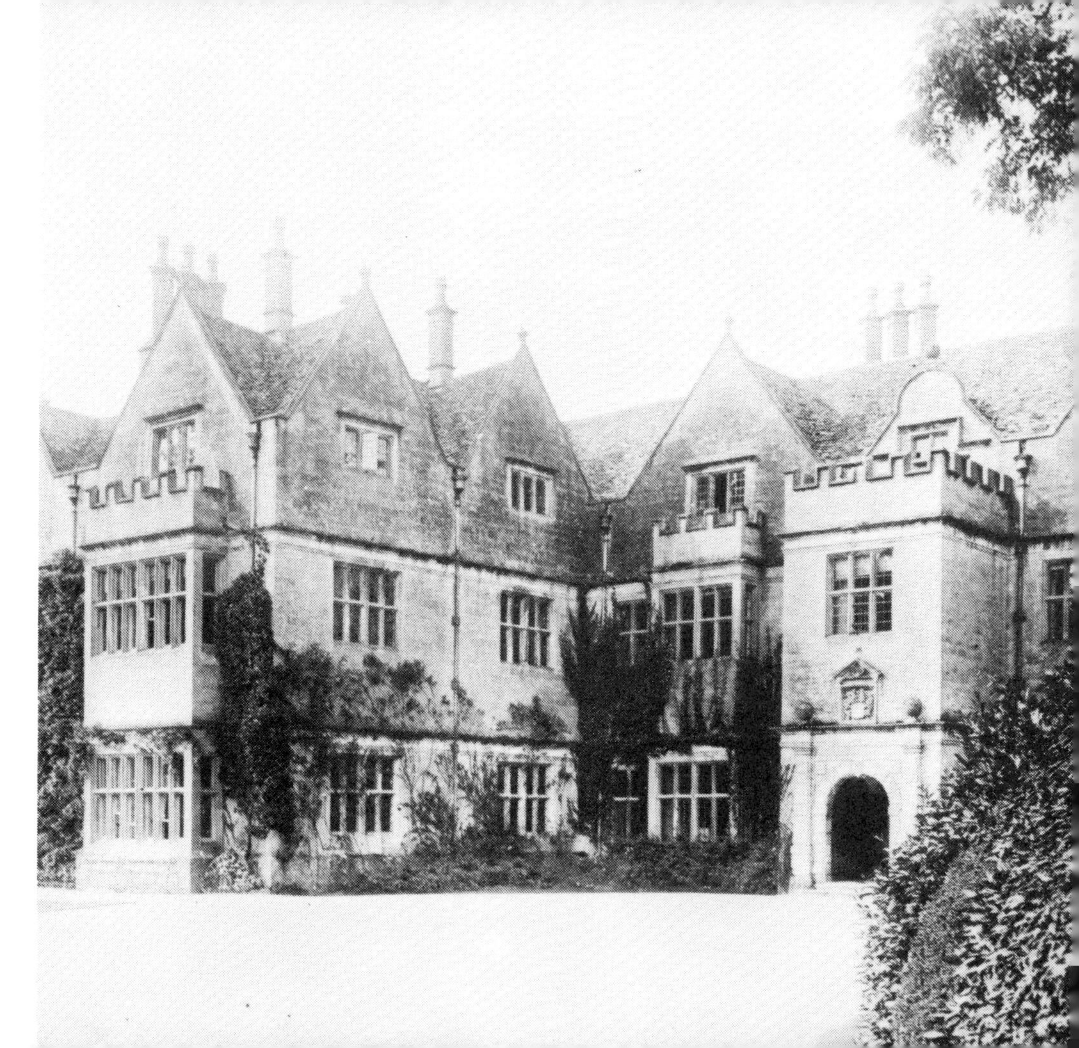

COMMERCE & SERVICES

For those living in the towns there were plenty of small shops providing for most daily needs and the shopkeeper kept long hours. Several family businesses survive today although modern pressures exact an increasing toll.

No. 9 In *Cirencester* until recently John Smith & Son traded in animal foodstuffs in Cricklade Street in the same premises as in this view c. 1905. The window display is a fascinating mixture of advertisements and goods.

No. 10 (far right) In the villages a solitary shop was usually the only source of supply although its range of goods catered for a wide variety of needs.

In addition, the mobile shop or delivery van proved a god-send and enabled fresh meat, for example, to be obtained from the butcher on a regular basis each week. Here the Chipping Norton family butcher's Henry Weston & Son deliver in *Kingham* village in the 1920's.

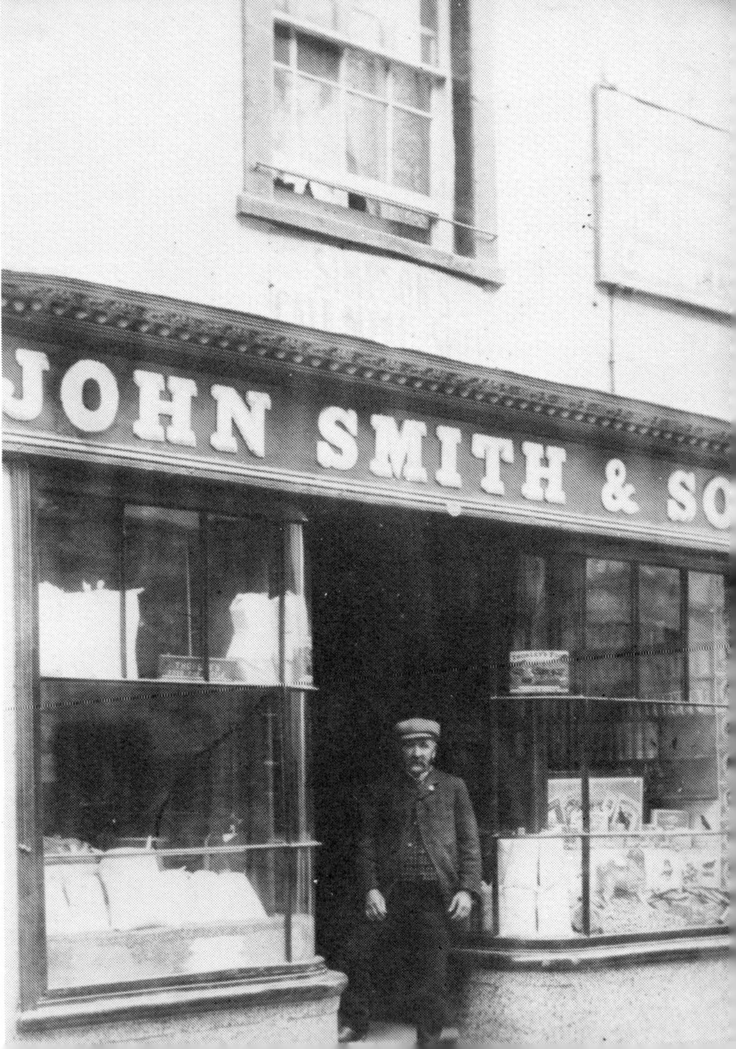

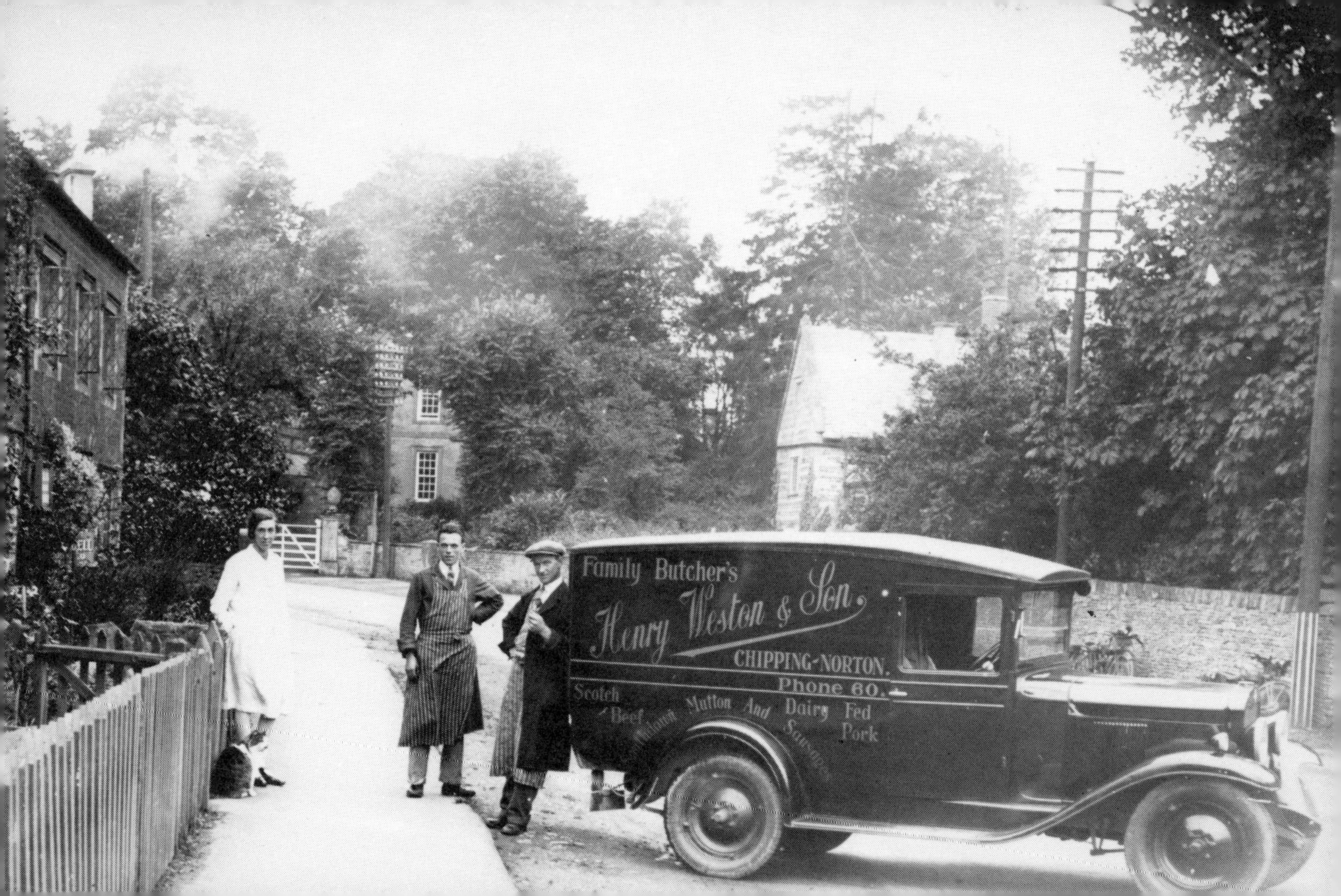
Family Butcher's
Henry Weston & Son
CHIPPING-NORTON.
Phone 60.
Scotch
Beef
Mutton And
Dairy Fed
Pork
Sausages

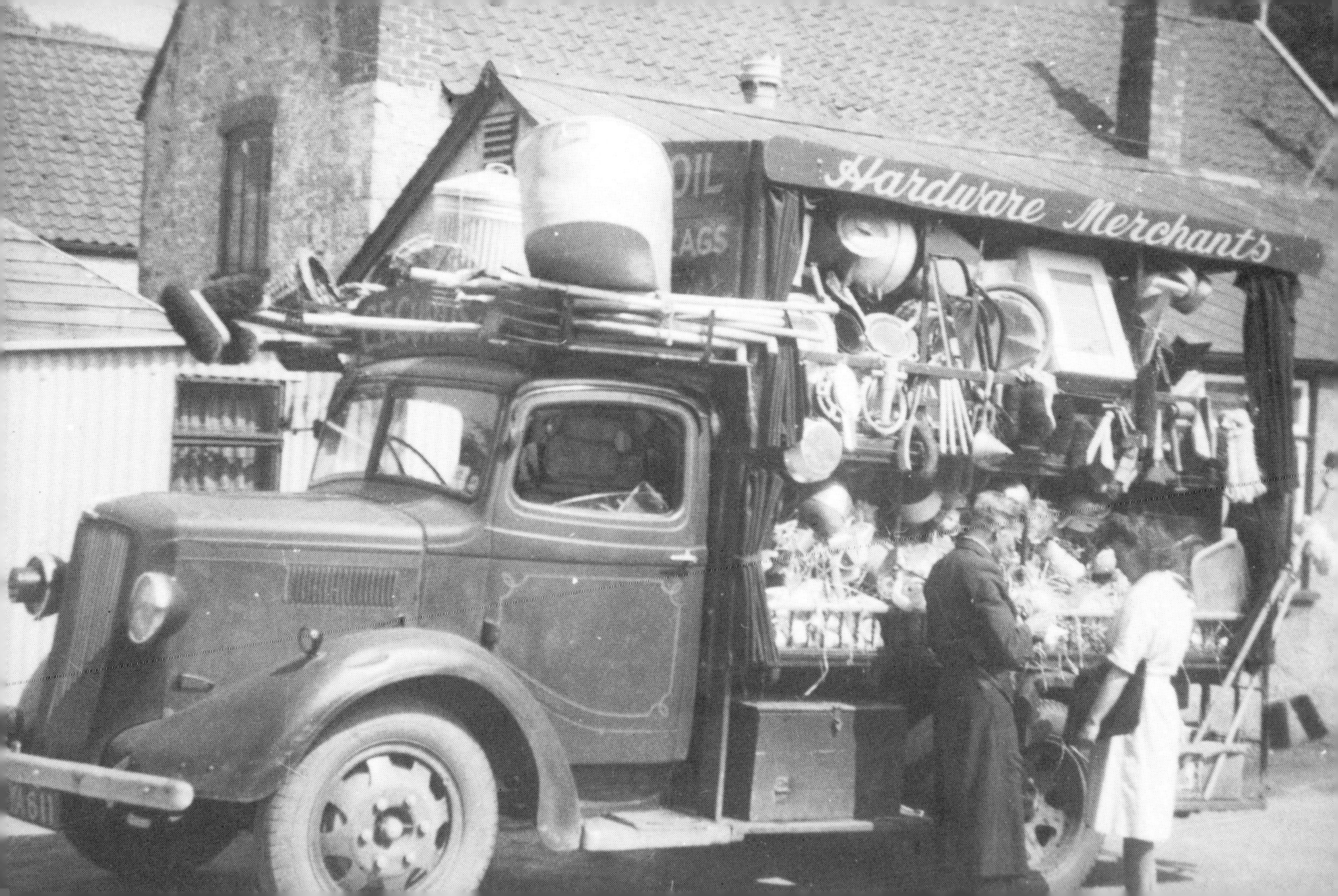
OIL
Hardware Merchants

No. 11 (left) The mobile shop remained a regular feature of country life until recent years when access to cars and better roads encouraged greater use of the nearby town for shopping. This mobile shop is a classic of its period; the photograph dates from 1947 and the village is (probably) *Lower Slaughter*. The van is full to the doors with an amazing variety of items, including even a zinc bath on the roof of the cab! Good humour and an ability to persist despite fluctuating trade and poor weather were basic requirements for the mobile shopkeeper.

Similar qualities were required by other country people travelling regularly around the district.

No. 12 (right) Mrs. Betty Smith, the district nurse at *Colesbourne,* with her own method of transport.

Nos. 13 & 14 (overleaf) Door-to-door delivery at *Willersey* near Broadway c. 1900. It is not clear what is being sold but it is heavy enough to require the use of a yoke.

Mr. G. Packer delivering milk in *Baunton* in the 1920's. He is riding a bicycle adapted to carry two cans of milk which was then ladled out at each delivery. The money bag hangs over the handlebars.

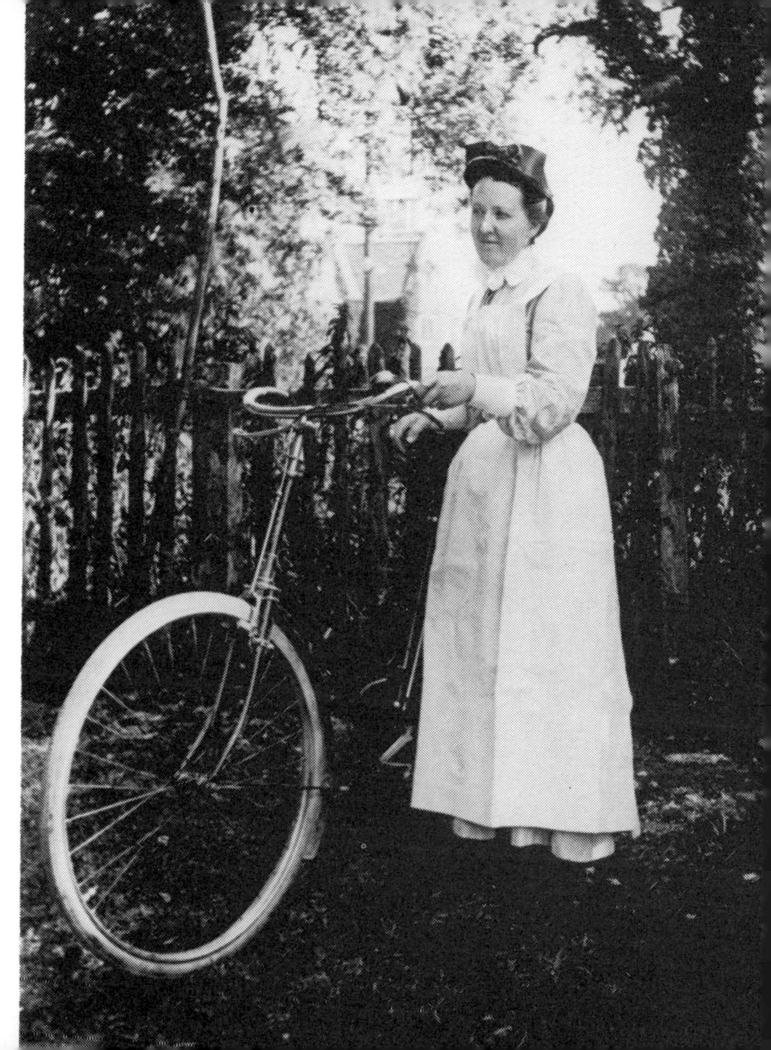

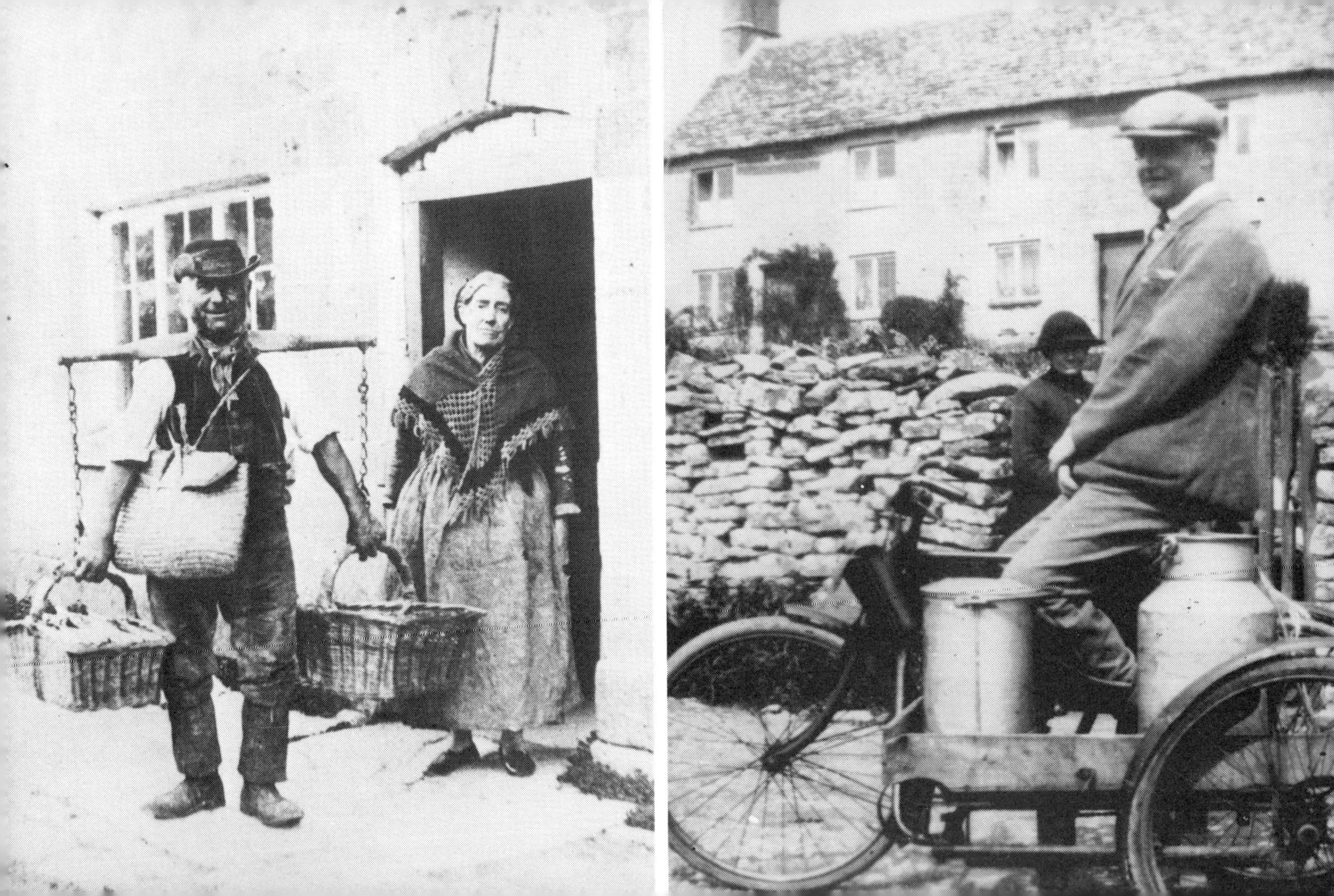

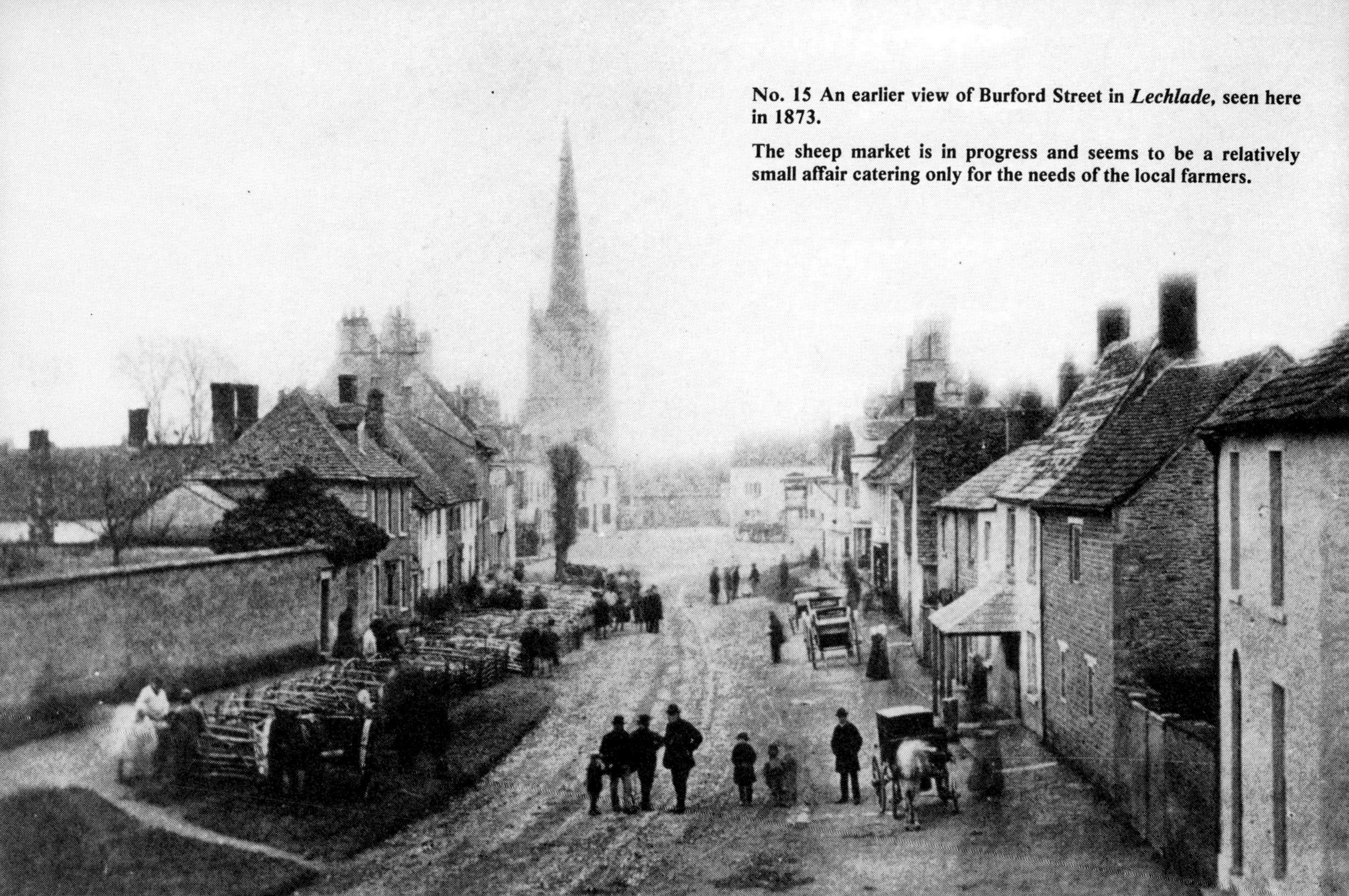

No. 15 An earlier view of Burford Street in *Lechlade,* seen here in 1873.

The sheep market is in progress and seems to be a relatively small affair catering only for the needs of the local farmers.

AGRICULTURE

No. 16 Oxen were popular on Gloucestershire farms and continued to be used for heavy work on the light hill soils long after the horse had superseded in other areas.

The last working team in the country survived at Cirencester Park until 1964 although latterly as celebrities rather than working beasts. This plough-team is probably on the Springhill estate near *Broadway* where oxen were regularly used until 1920.

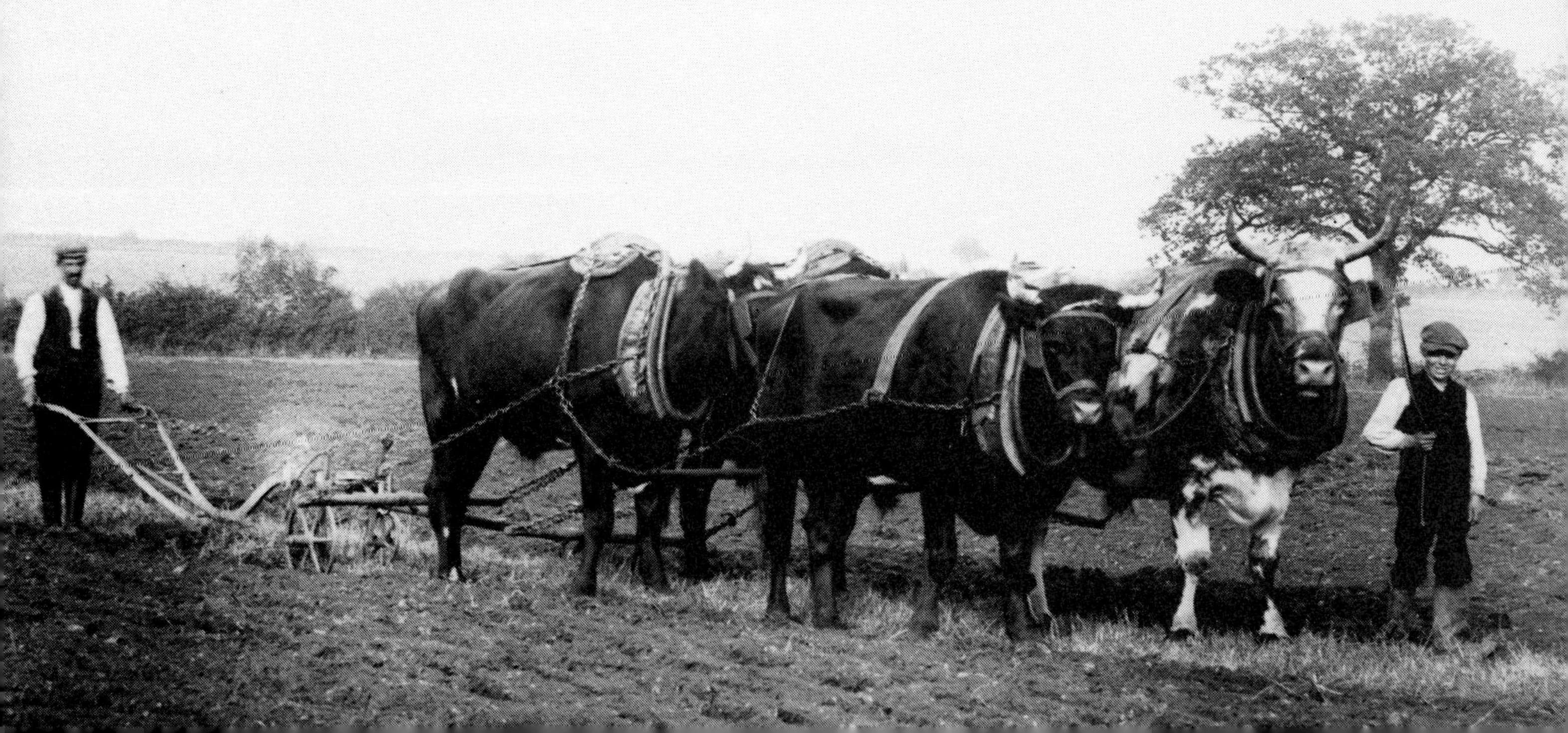

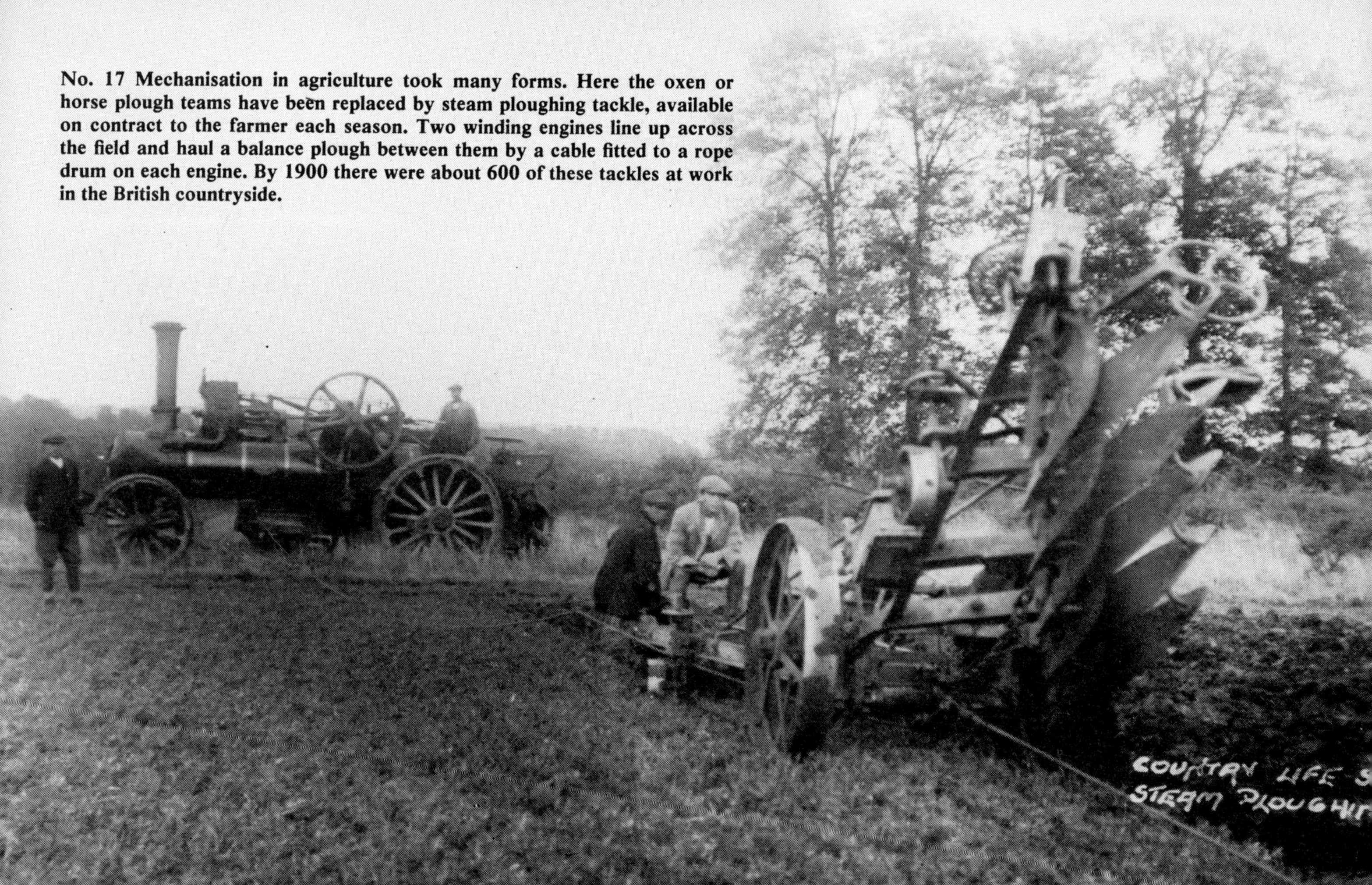

No. 17 Mechanisation in agriculture took many forms. Here the oxen or horse plough teams have been replaced by steam ploughing tackle, available on contract to the farmer each season. Two winding engines line up across the field and haul a balance plough between them by a cable fitted to a rope drum on each engine. By 1900 there were about 600 of these tackles at work in the British countryside.

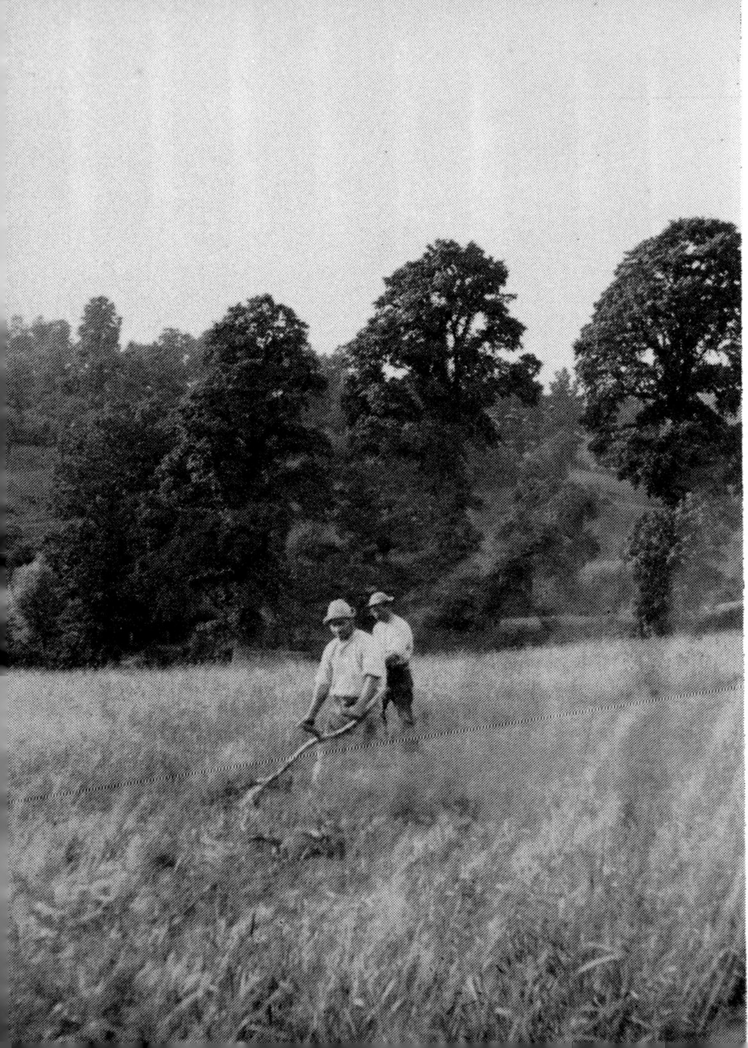

No. 18 Mowing by hand before the adoption of machinery. Hand mowing such as this at Sheephouse, *Painswick* in July 1905 survived in fields too steep for machines or where no machinery was available.

Haymaking was a time of long hours of labour in the fields, often fondly remembered today as a happy time in early summer when community effort was required to gather in the hay while the weather was fair. It was also an opportunity to earn a little more money for extra effort.

Nos. 19 (opposite) & 20 (overleaf) The harvest was equally exacting. Here the crop is gathered in loosely from the field in a harvest waggon for the journey to the rick which might be in the corner of the field or one of a group in the farmyard, as seen here clustered around the farm buildings.

No. 21 (overleaf) Two old men at *Southrop* near Lechlade in 1904 who were no doubt passing the time of day with the farm worker behind when the opportunity occurred to be photographed. Comments on the advantages of the older methods of farming seem always to have dominated such wayside conversations.

Nos. 19–21 probably form part of a group taken near Lechlade by the photographer and are thus almost contemporary. The waggon, boy and rear oxen in No. 19 appear again in No. 20 and the labourer in No. 20 again in No. 21. Fyfield is close by Southrop.

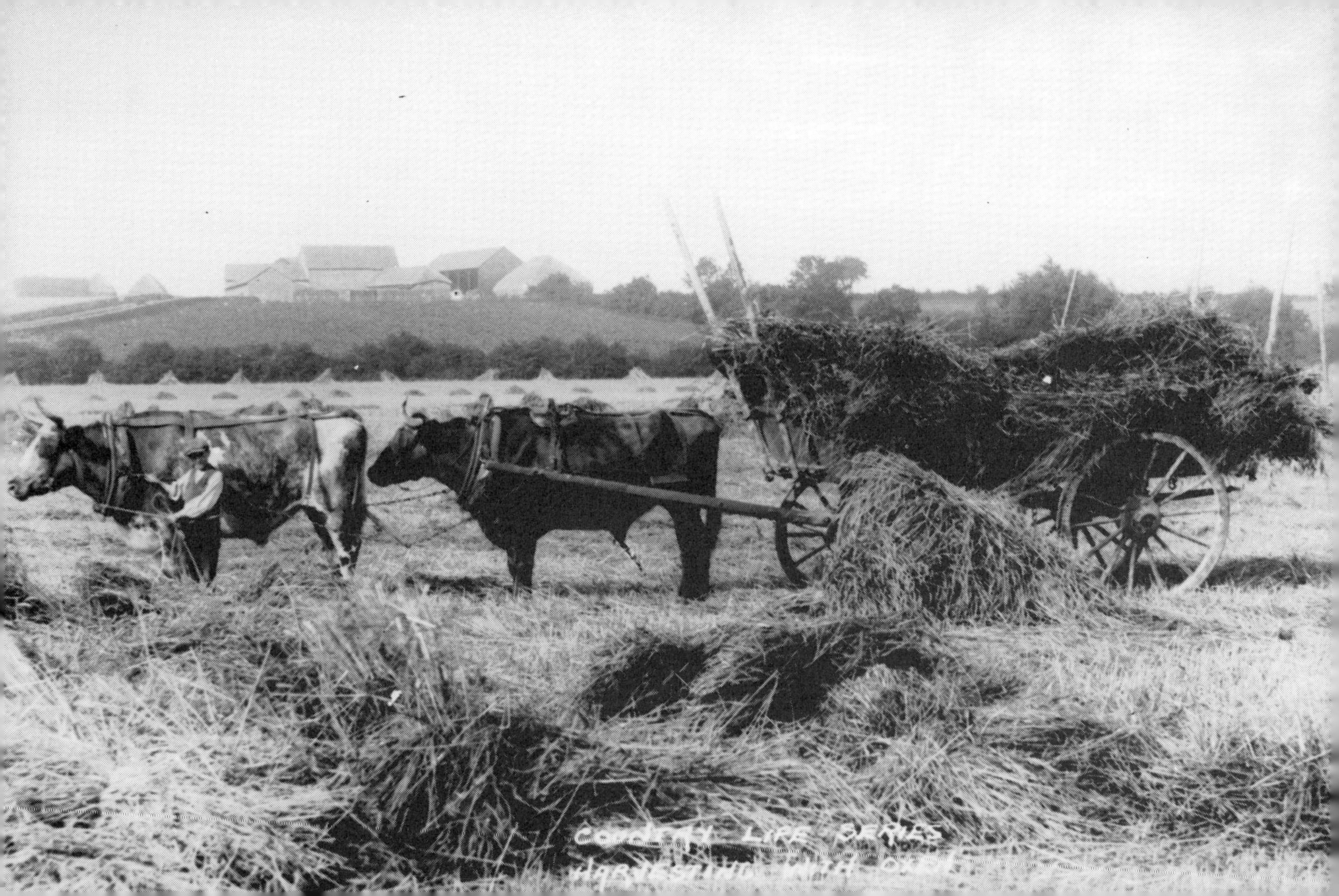
COUNTRY LIFE SERIES
HARVESTING WITH OXEN

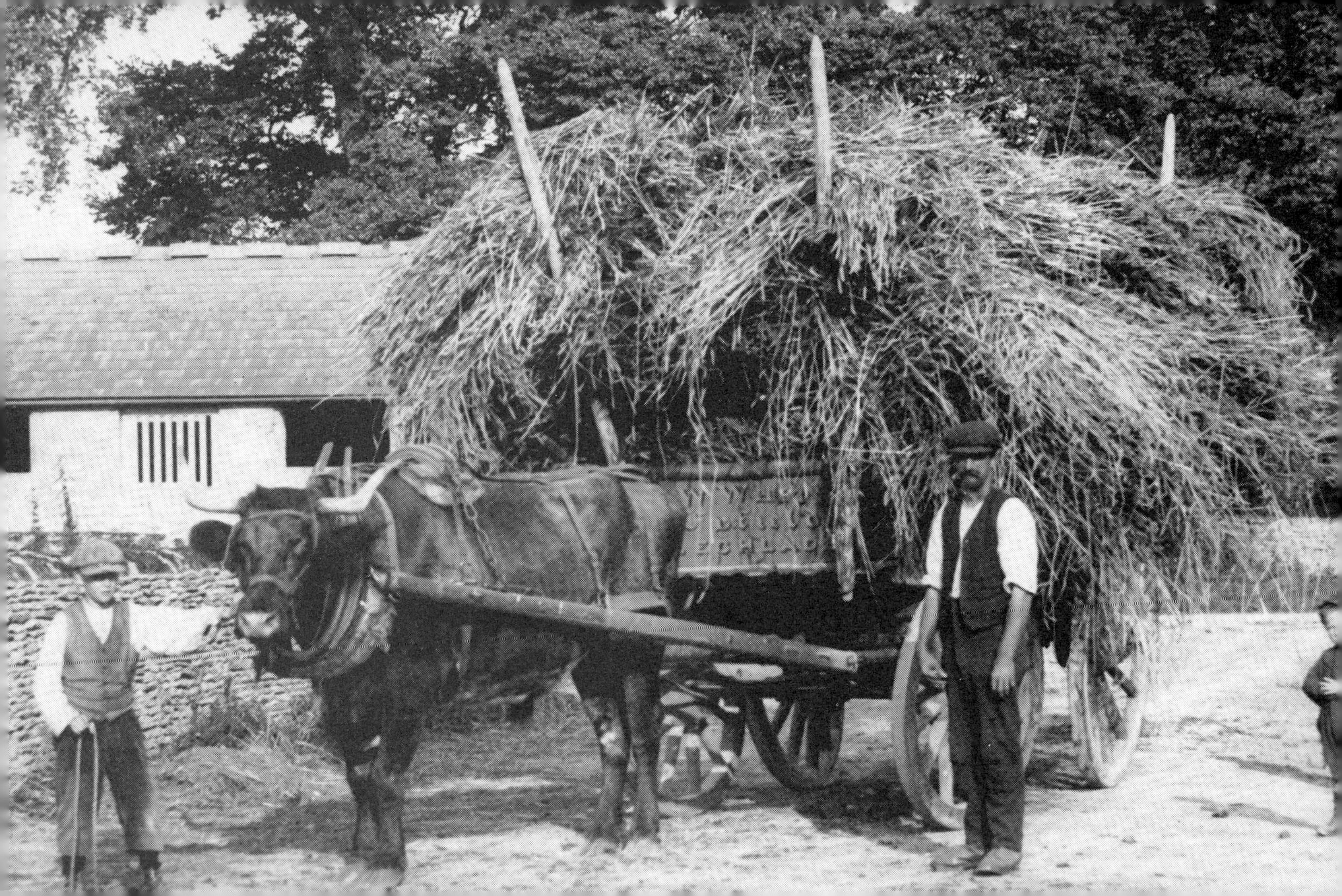

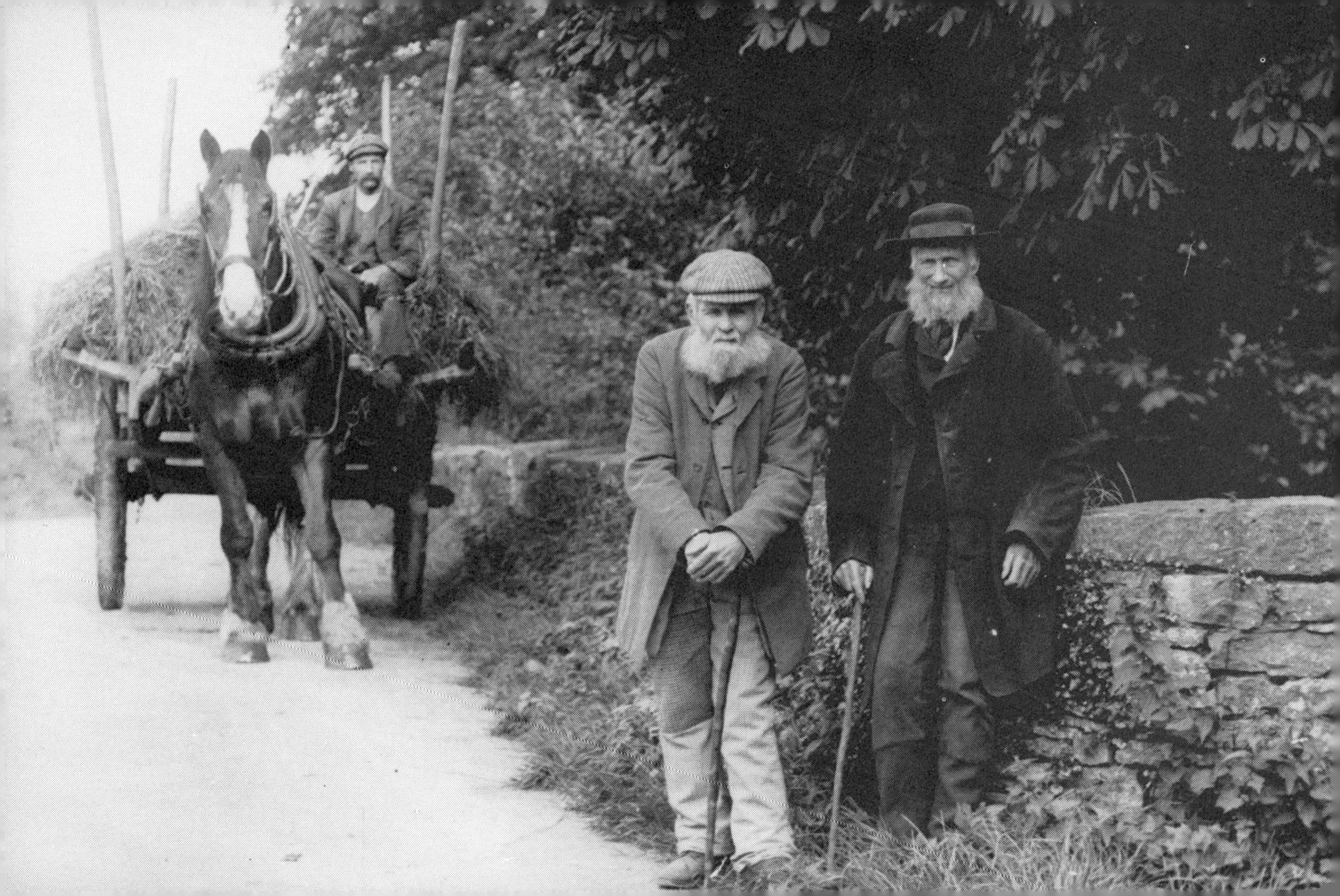

No. 22 When required for winter feed for animals, hay was removed from the rick. In this view during the First World War, the hay is being 'pressed' or baled using steam power. The Forage Department of the Army Service Corps included many men with agricultural or traction engine experience.

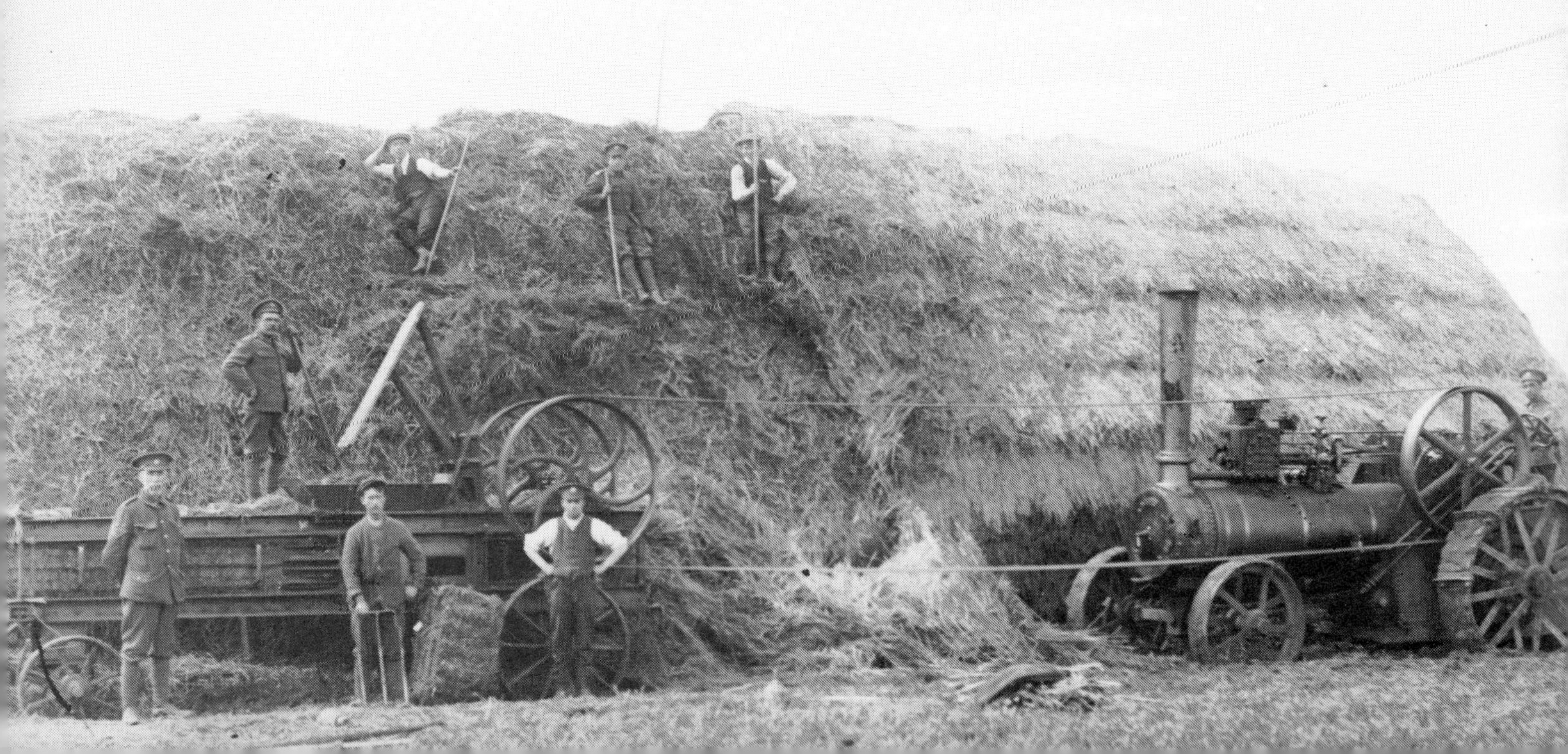

No. 23 Reaper-binders at work during the harvest on an unidentified Cotswold farm. The day's work here is nearly over – the field has been cut and the sheaves of corn 'stooked' ready for threshing.

Nos. 24 & 25 (overleaf) The threshing activity in the farmyard. These are different scenes but probably almost contemporary; note the untidiness of one and the ultra-efficiency of the other.

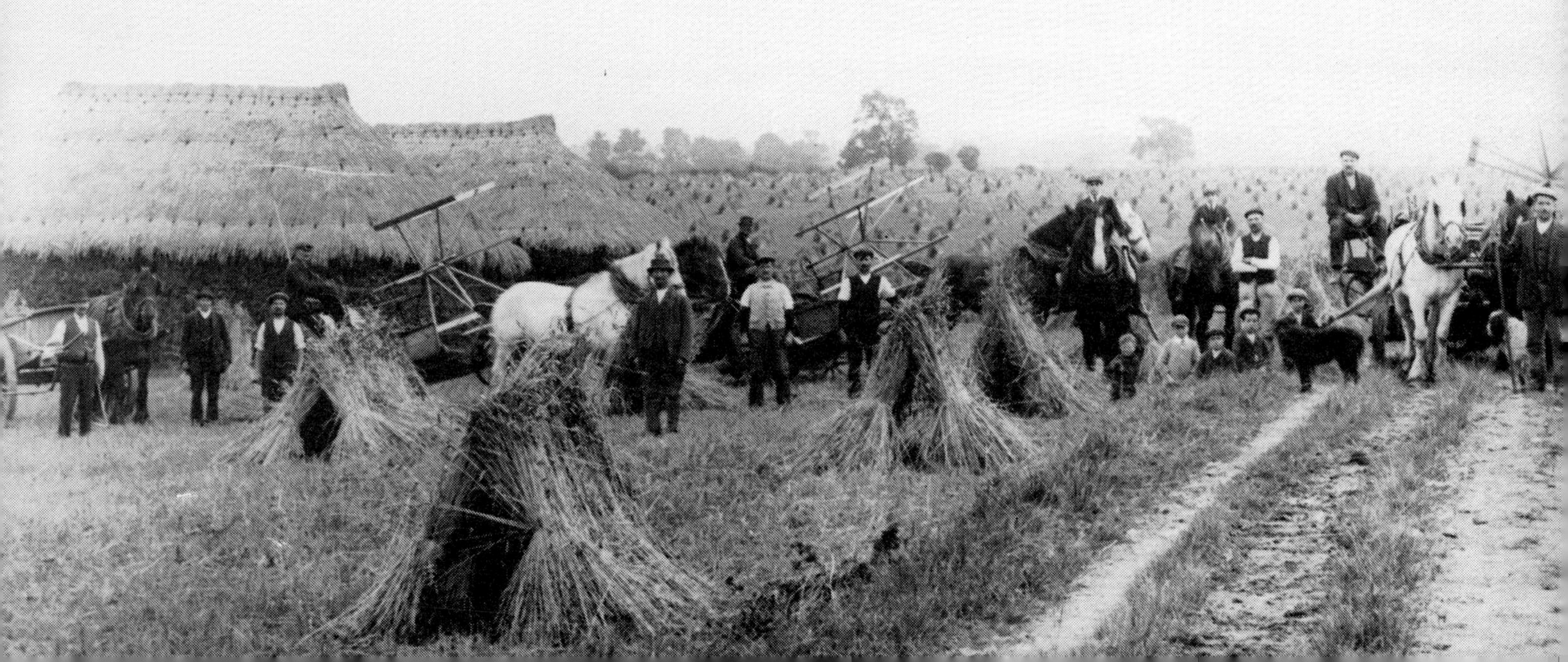

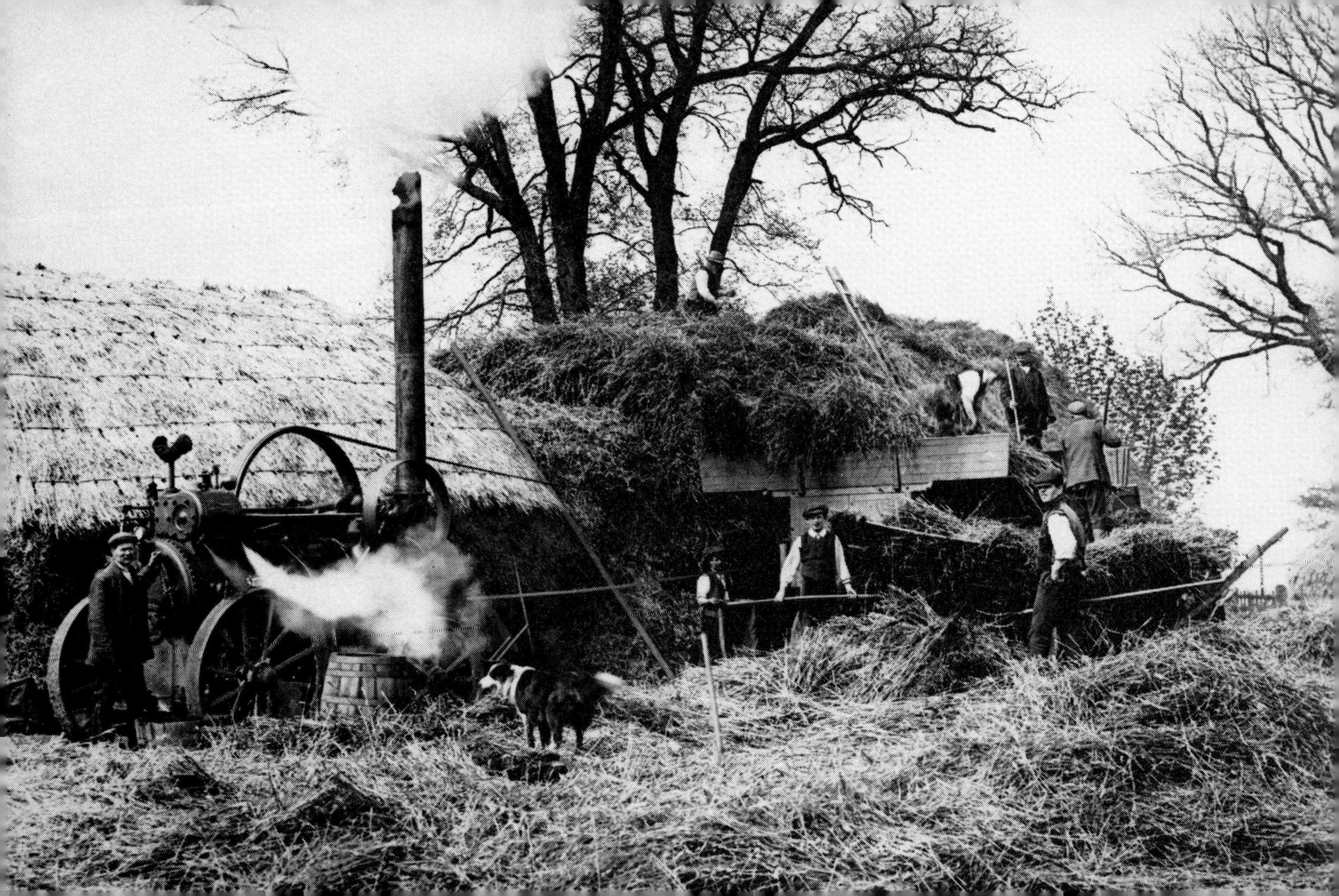

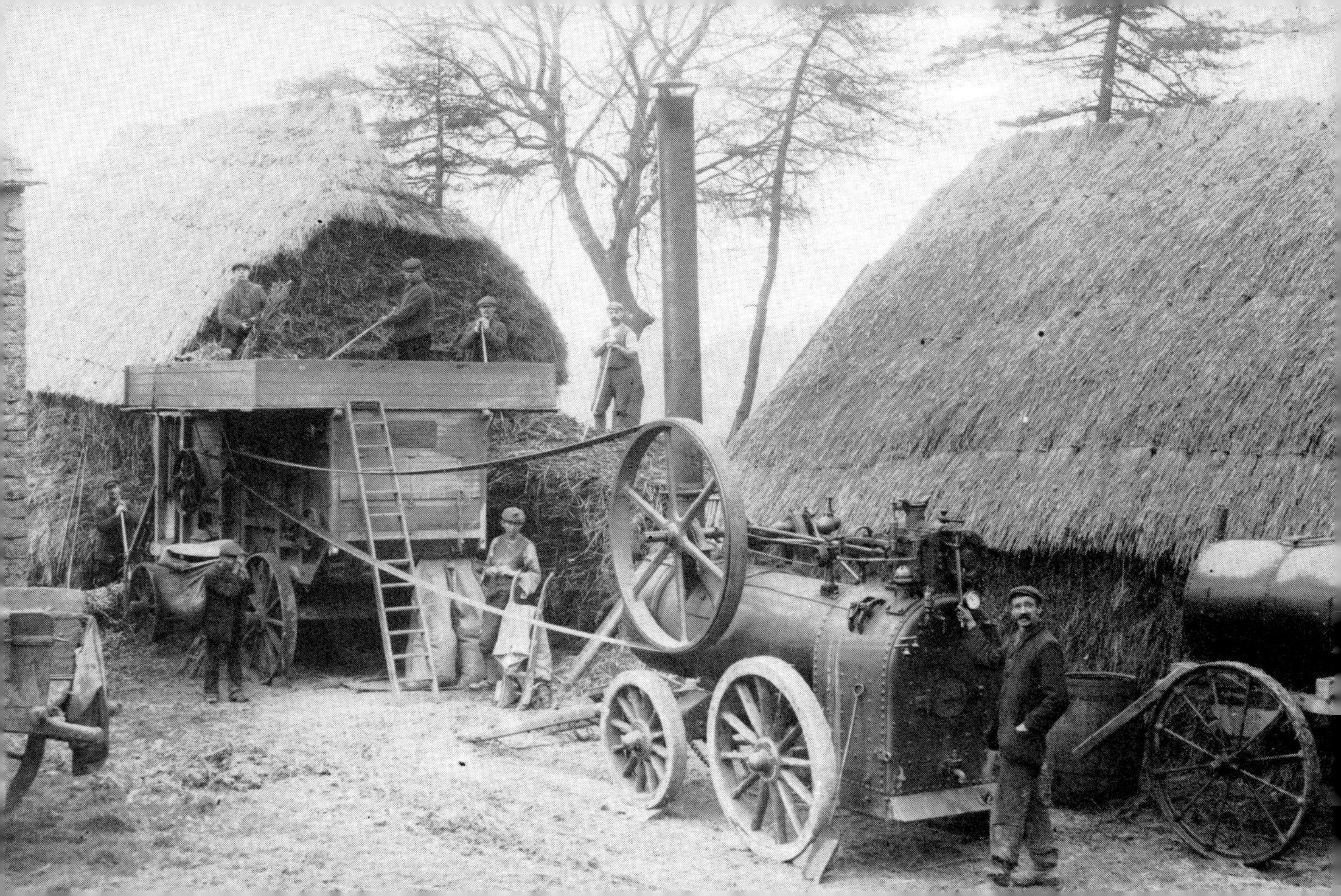

COTSWOLD STONE

The Cotswold hills are littered with small quarries mostly now overgrown and hidden from sight. The limestone has always been much sought-after as a building stone and is still quarried in a few places on a commercial scale. Nowadays its use is largely in restoration work of Cotswold houses or as an ingredient in reconstituted stone or roadstone.

No. 26 (right) Westington quarry above *Chipping Campden* seen here c. 1895. From this quarry came much of the stone for the building of Campden; this view shows the entrance on the left to the mine workings from which stone was extracted by means of a railway. Note the stone blocks stacked up around the crane. It was the custom to sell stone by the yard and to store different types of stone separately in the quarry, keeping walling stone, for example, apart from building stone. In the background, the stratification of the bed-rock shows clearly.

Nos. 27 & 28 (overleaf) Apart from building stone, Cotswold limestone also produces excellent roofing material and it is arguably the roofs of Cotswold buildings which establish their character as much as the buildings themselves. The most famous source of roofing material was Stonesfield in Oxfordshire where village life was dominated by the industry, but tiles or slates were also produced from tile pits in many villages.

This is Eyford quarry at *Naunton,* showing the roughly-hewn slates stacked up in the field by the quarry and being split with a slate hammer. After weathering, the slates were then shaped using a 'crapping stone' set upon the ground to achieve the right shape and thickness; the peg hole was made with another special tool known as a slat-pick.

Each size of slate had its own particular name and on the Cotswolds there are several fascinating variations from one district to another.

Drystone walling is another distinguishing feature of the Cotswold landscape and it too has a long tradition. Walling as a profession is now reviving although many of its traditional characteristics have changed.

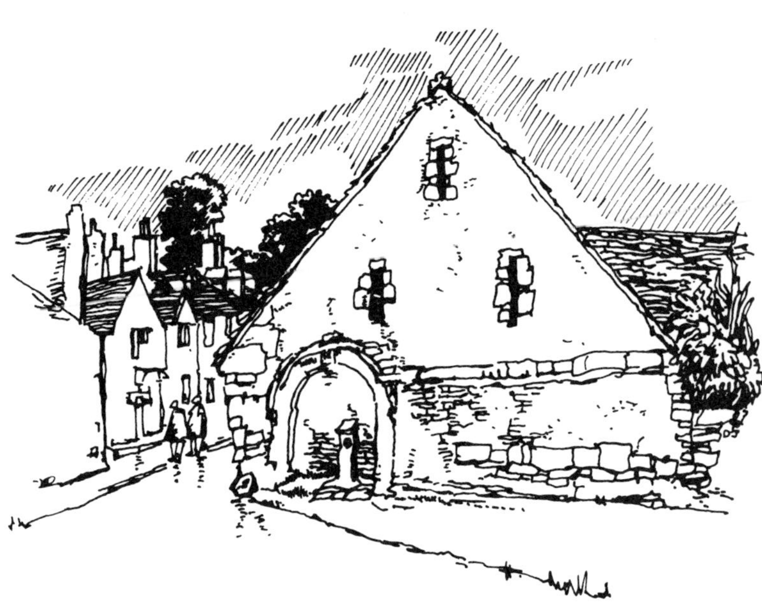

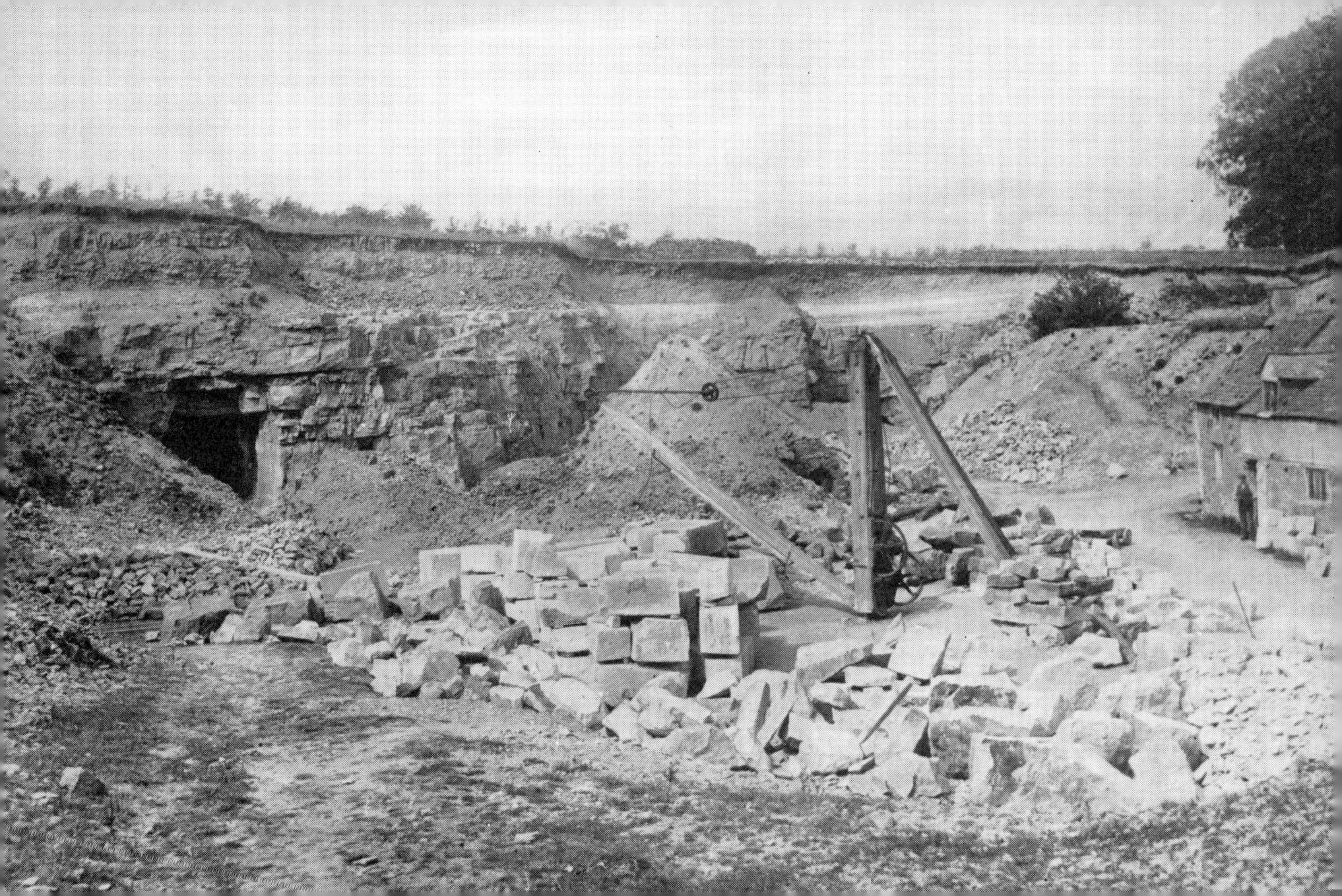

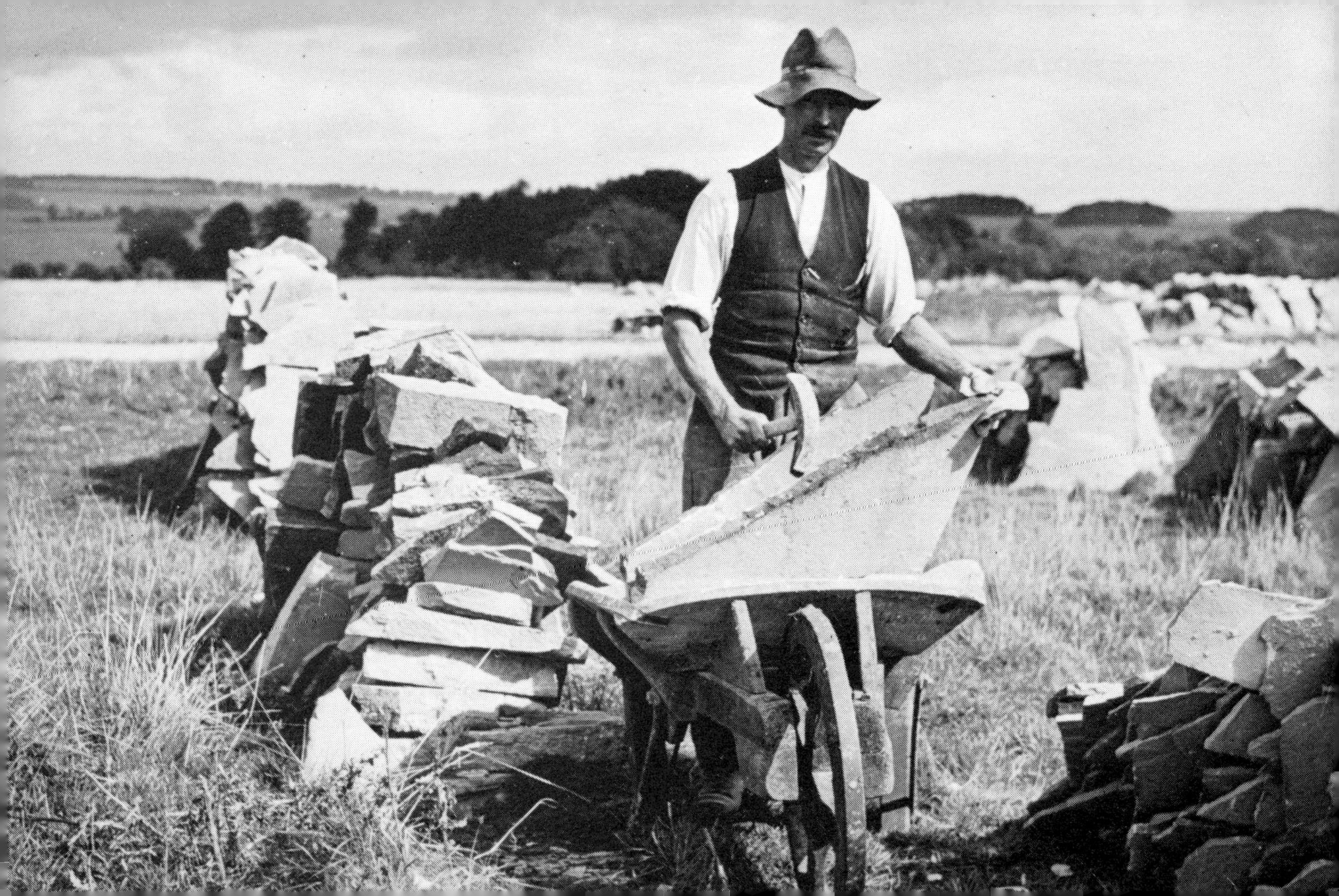

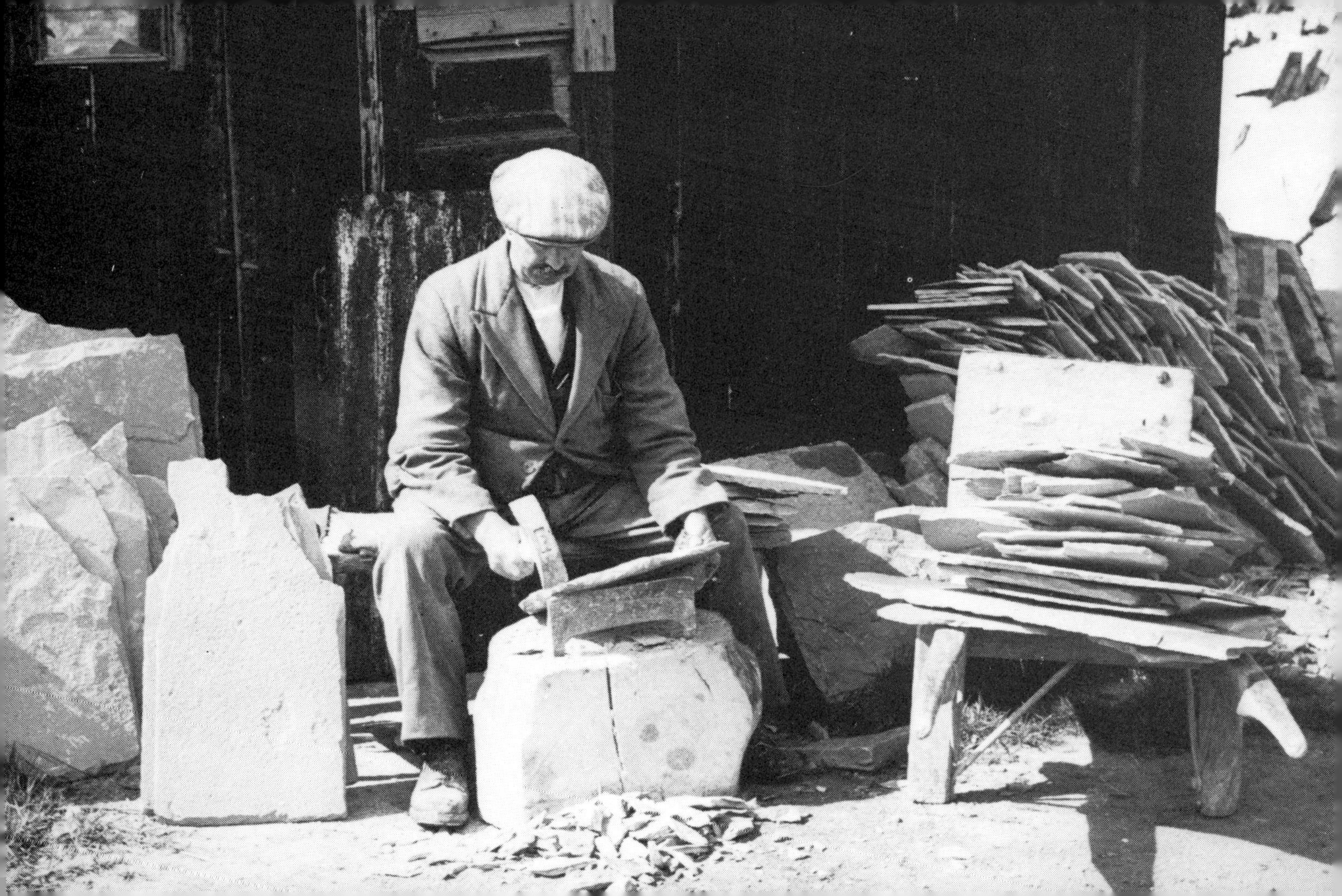

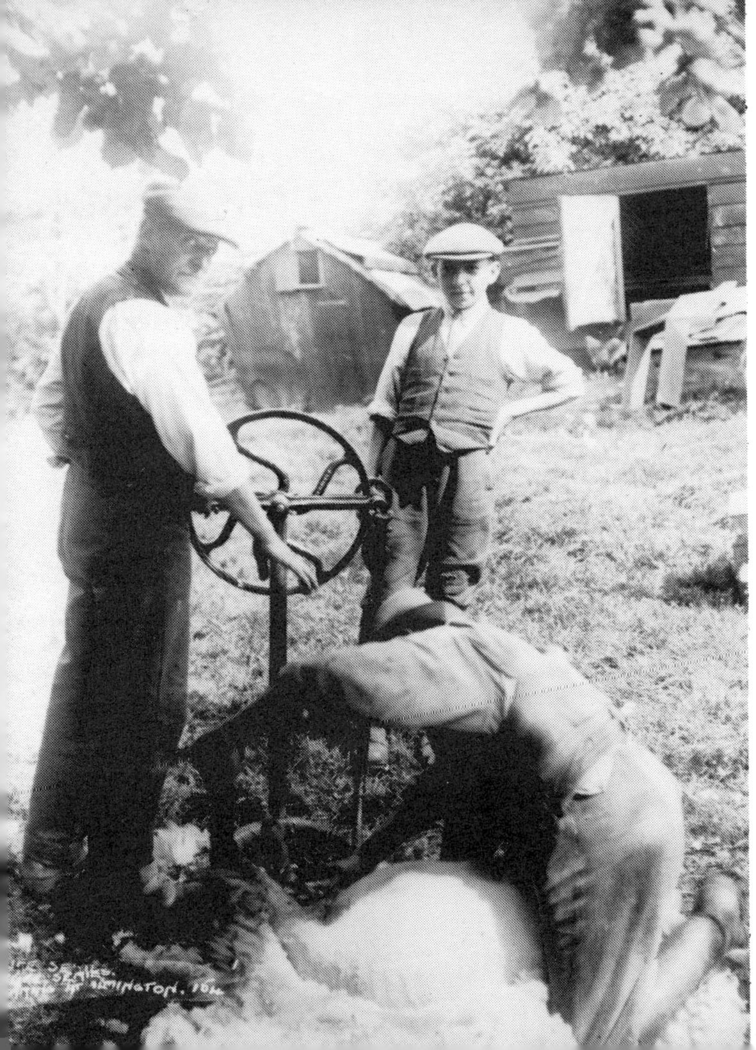

CRAFTS & TRADES

Country life was reliant upon the availability of a broad range of skills, usually to be found within the local community. Each village required its blacksmith and wheelwright and the agricultural cycle absorbed any casual labour which might be available at busy times of the year. Children seem always to have been on hand to watch and to hope for a small task to perform.

No. 29 Sheep-shearing at *Ilmington,* Warwickshire in the 1920's. A portable shearing-machine is being used and powered by hand. The sheep is held down by the shearer with its neck between his knees. Such portable clippers were in common use in farmyards as well as in the fields.

No. 30 (right) The miller was particularly important to the local community and the mill was usually a scene of considerable activity.

This is *Bourton on the Water* corn mill in the centre of the village, seen here between the wars.

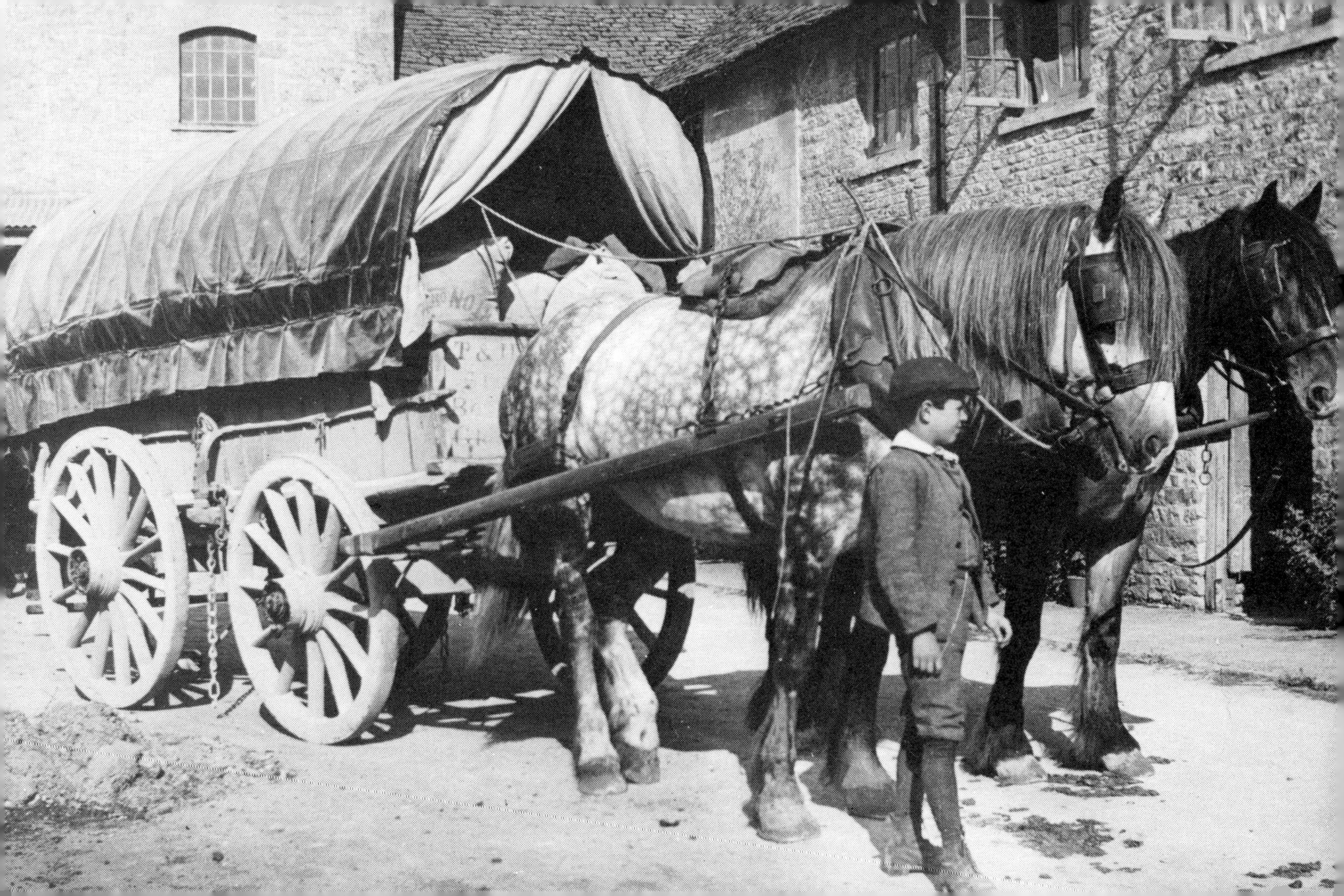

No. 31 (below) The village blacksmith at *Kingham* with his (no doubt) customary audience. Note the flag-stone wall and the mass of stored horseshoes.

No. 32 (right) Clutter with a purpose in Tom Whiting's wheelwright's shop at *Bourton-on-the-Water*.

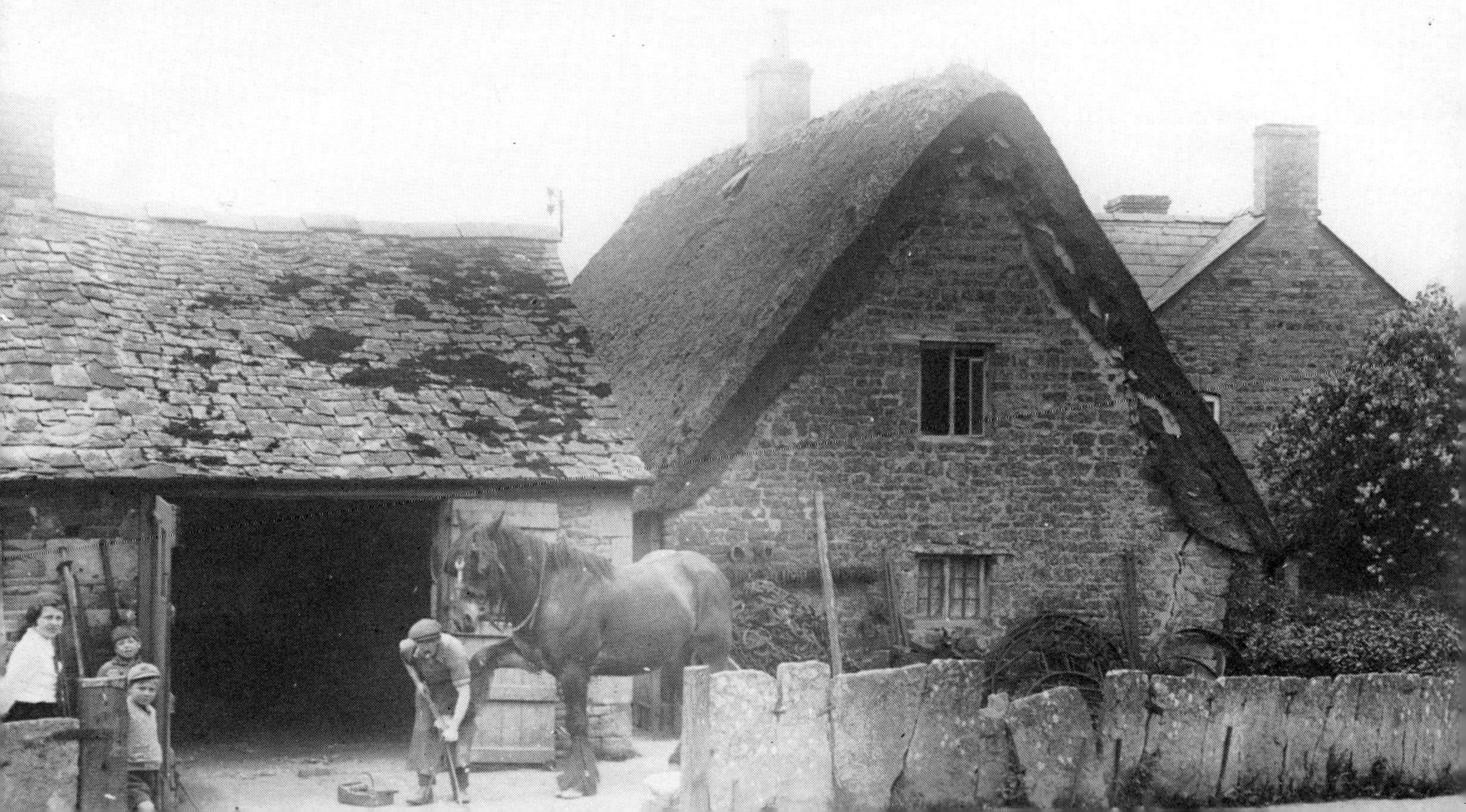

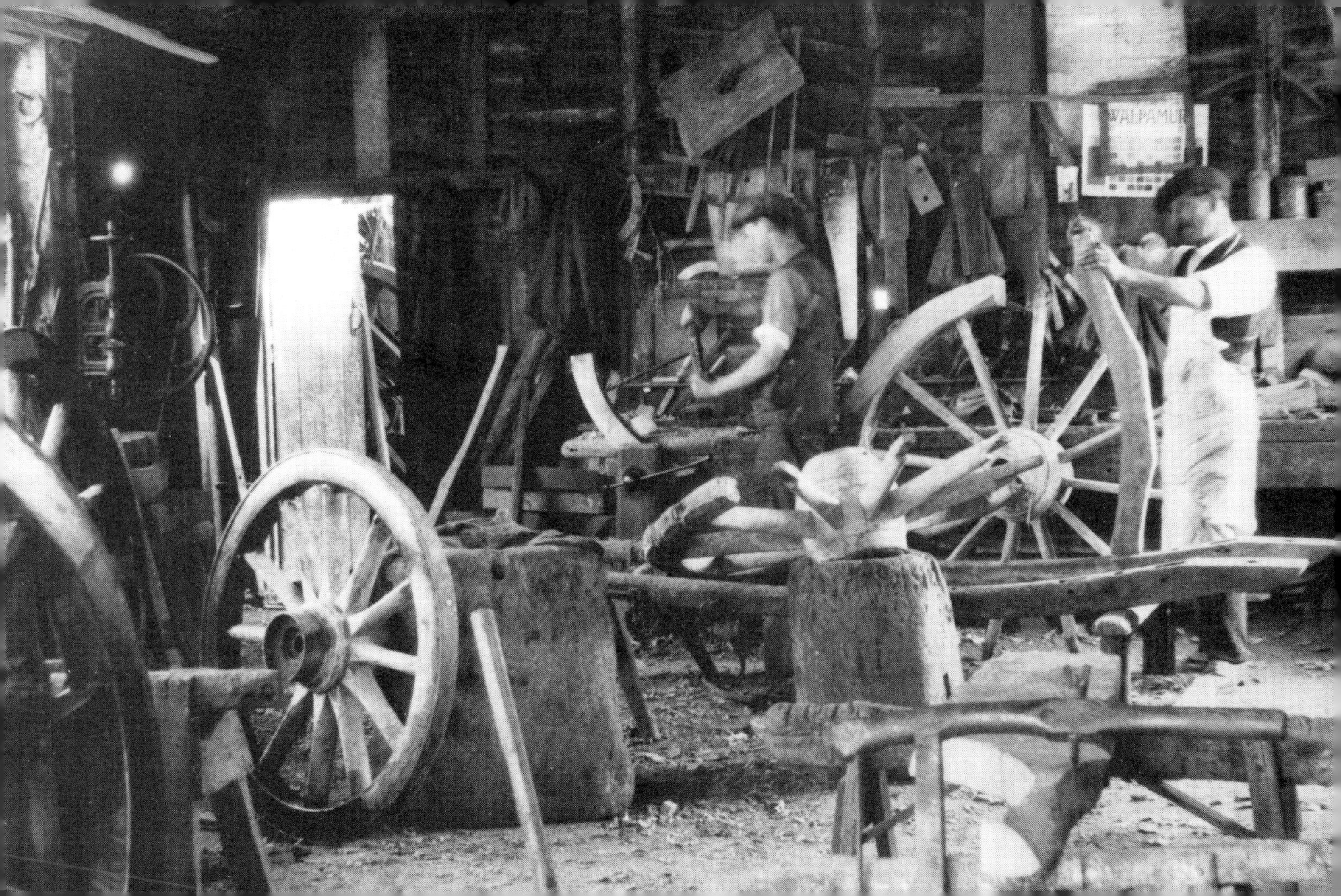
WALPAMUR

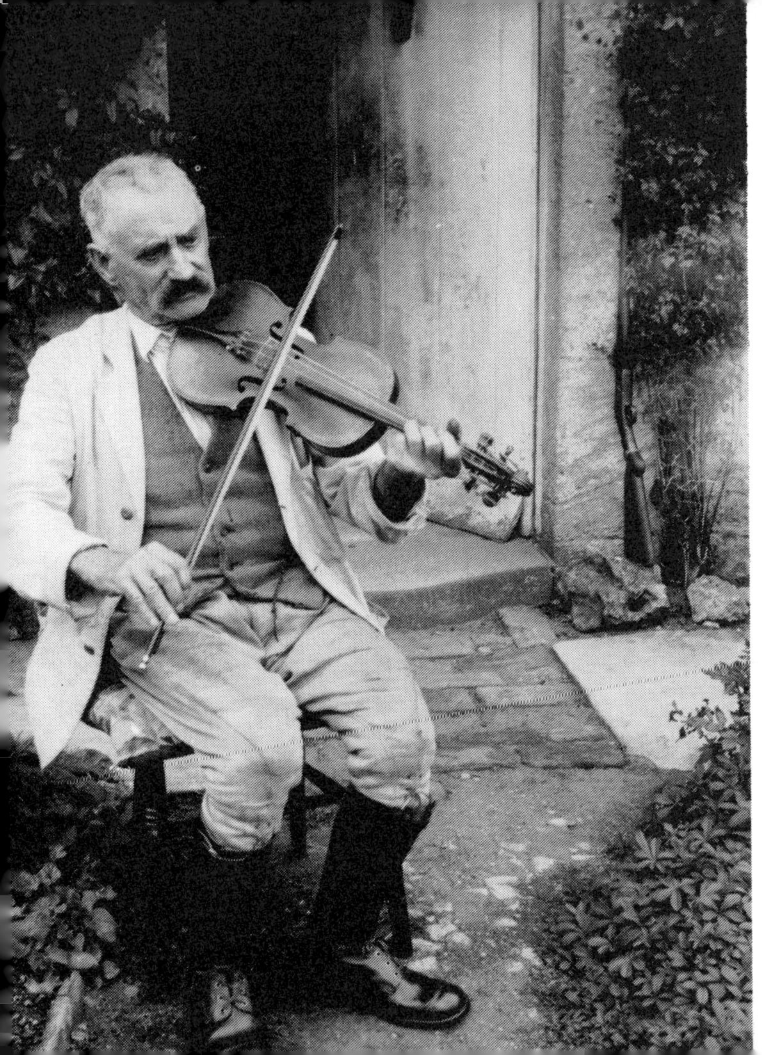

TRADITIONS & EVENTS

No. 33 (left) Thomas Hardy described the church musicians in 'Under the Greenwood Tree' in the days before harmonium and organ. This church fiddler in a Cotswold village continued the tradition but only in the absence of a harmonium player!

No. 34 (right) Probably the best known local tradition is morris dancing, a time-honoured association of Cotswold villages with groups or 'sides' of men dancing on village occasions. Whitsun was (and still is) the traditional time for this activity and each village with its own side would boast a special day and a 'tradition' of dances peculiar to itself. Here are the *Headington Quarry* morris men outside the Chequers Inn in 1898.

No. 35 (overleaf) Club-day was perhaps the major item on the village social calendar, when all the village paraded with the local band. The church parade, as here at *Bampton* c. 1905, was followed by a generous dinner in the local pub to which the men had subscribed through a 'club'. In many villages the festivities lasted for three days.

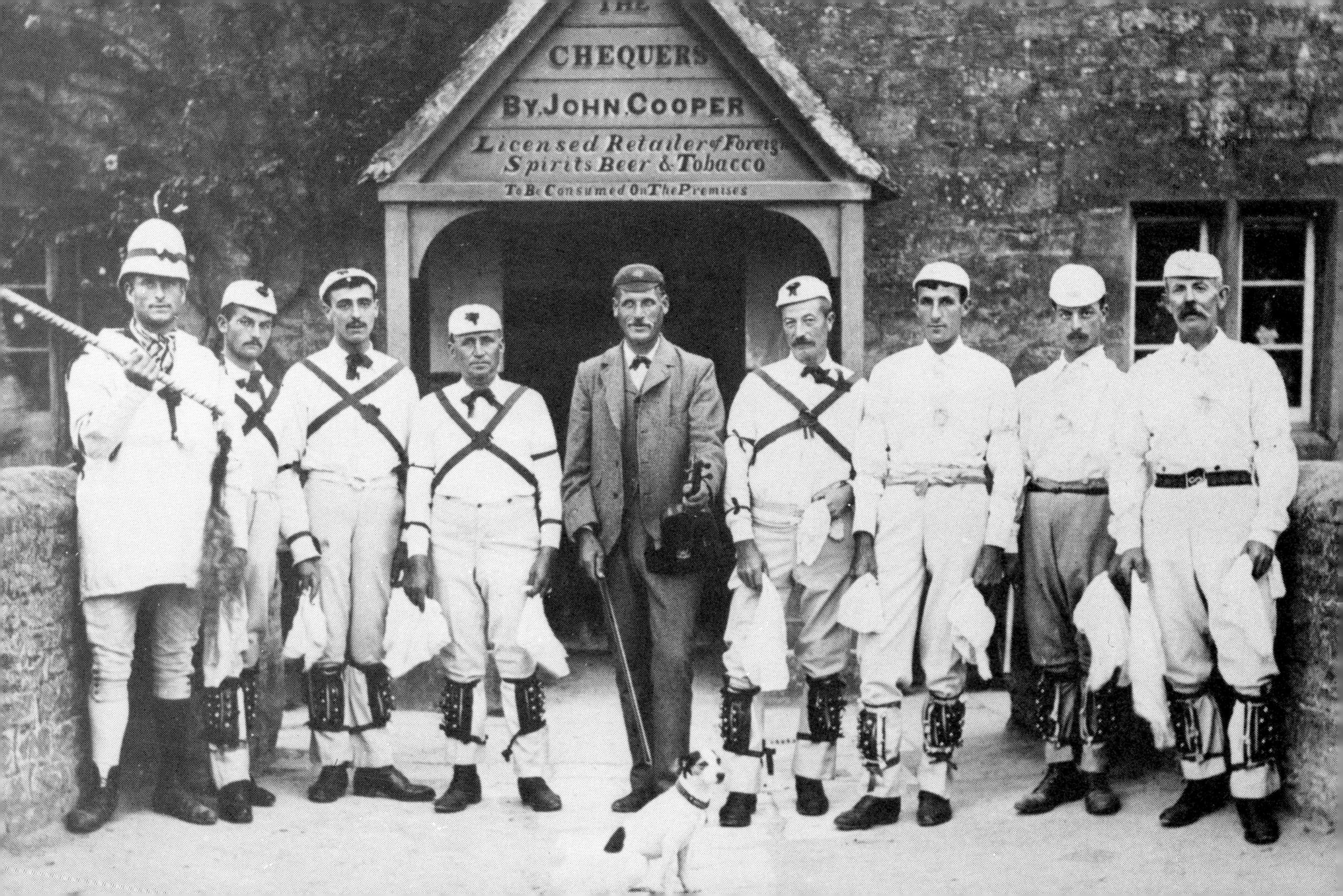
CHEQUERS
BY. JOHN. COOPER
Licensed Retailer of Foreign
Spirits Beer & Tobacco
To Be Consumed On The Premises

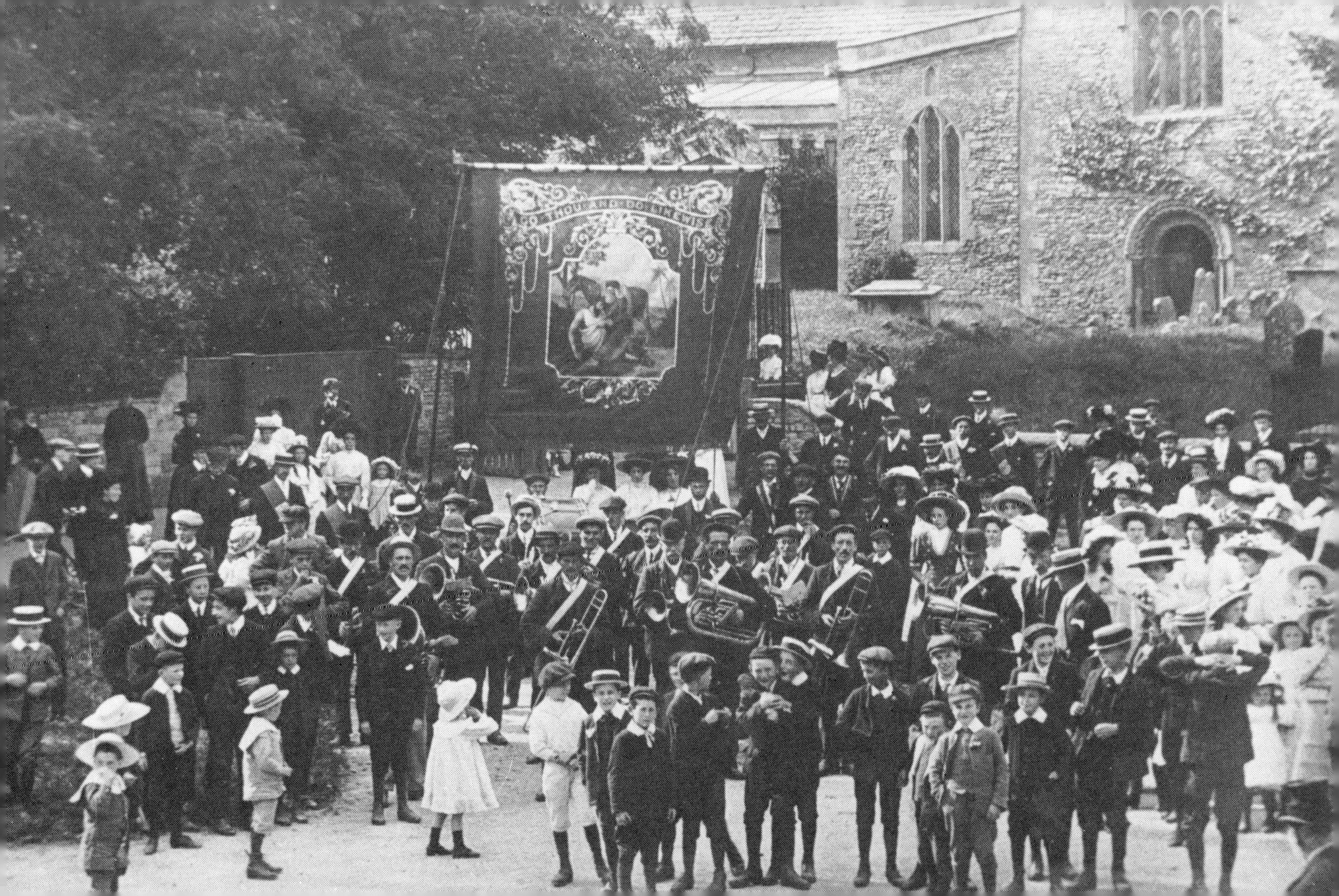

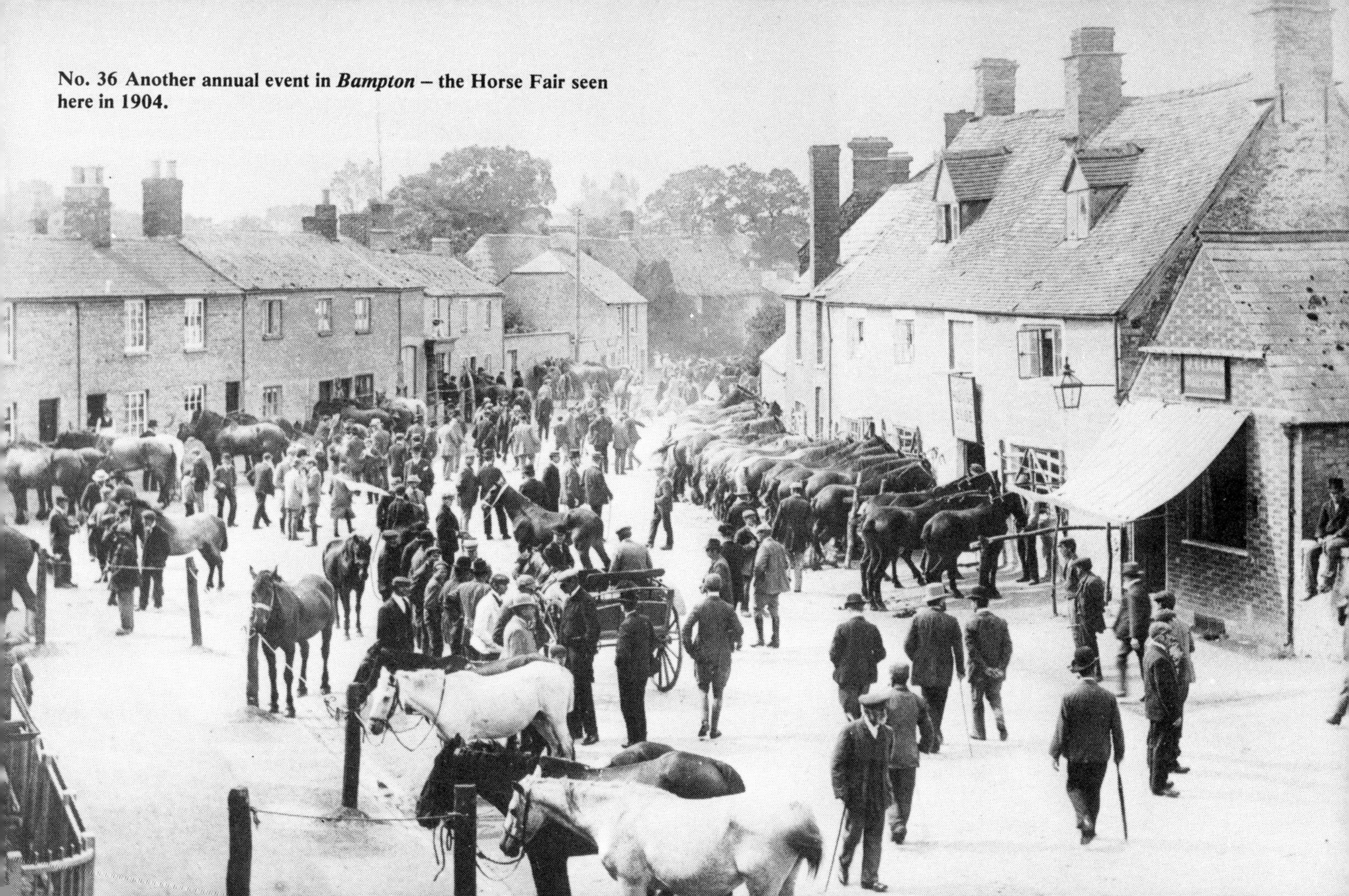

No. 36 Another annual event in *Bampton* – the Horse Fair seen here in 1904.

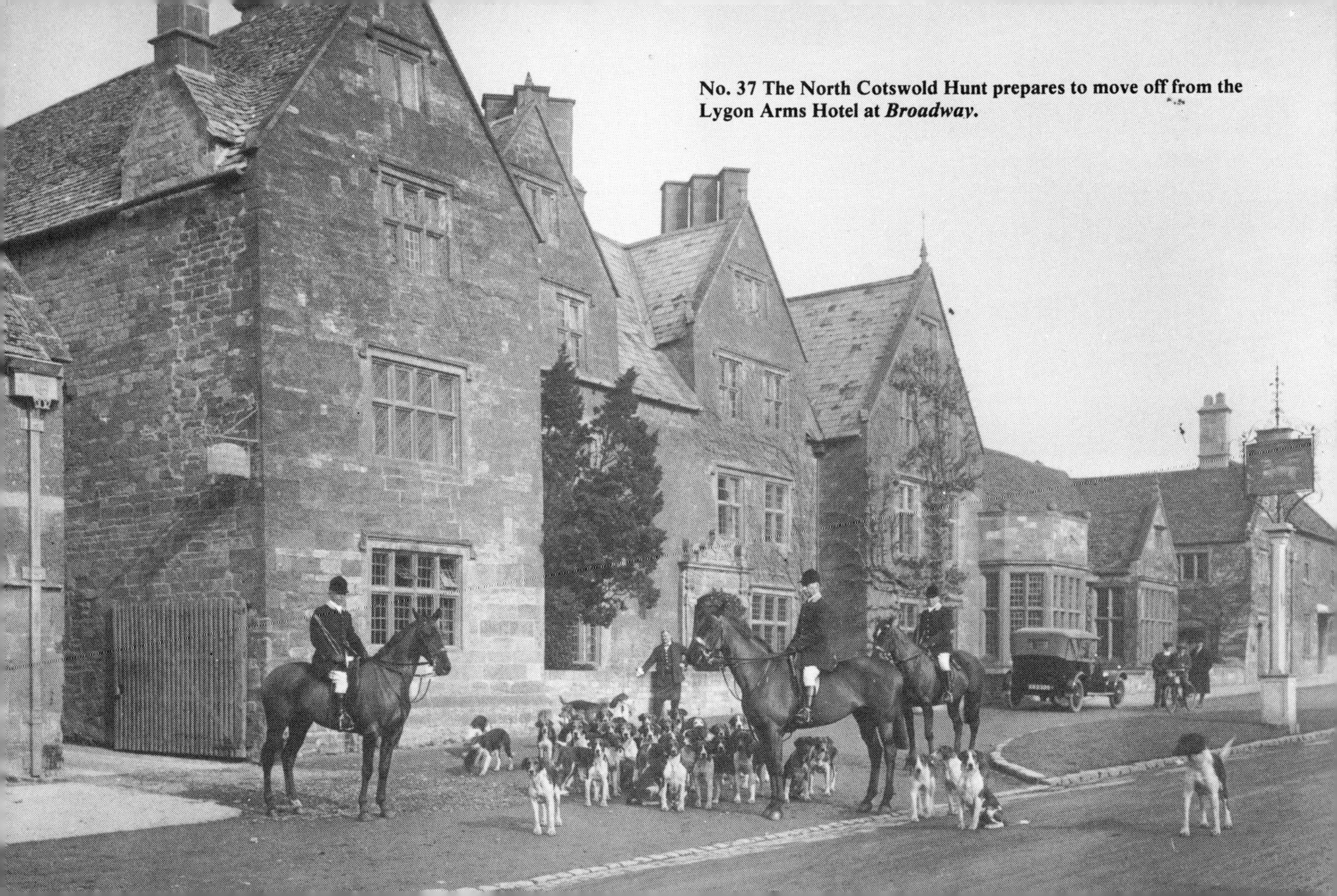
No. 37 The North Cotswold Hunt prepares to move off from the Lygon Arms Hotel at ***Broadway.***

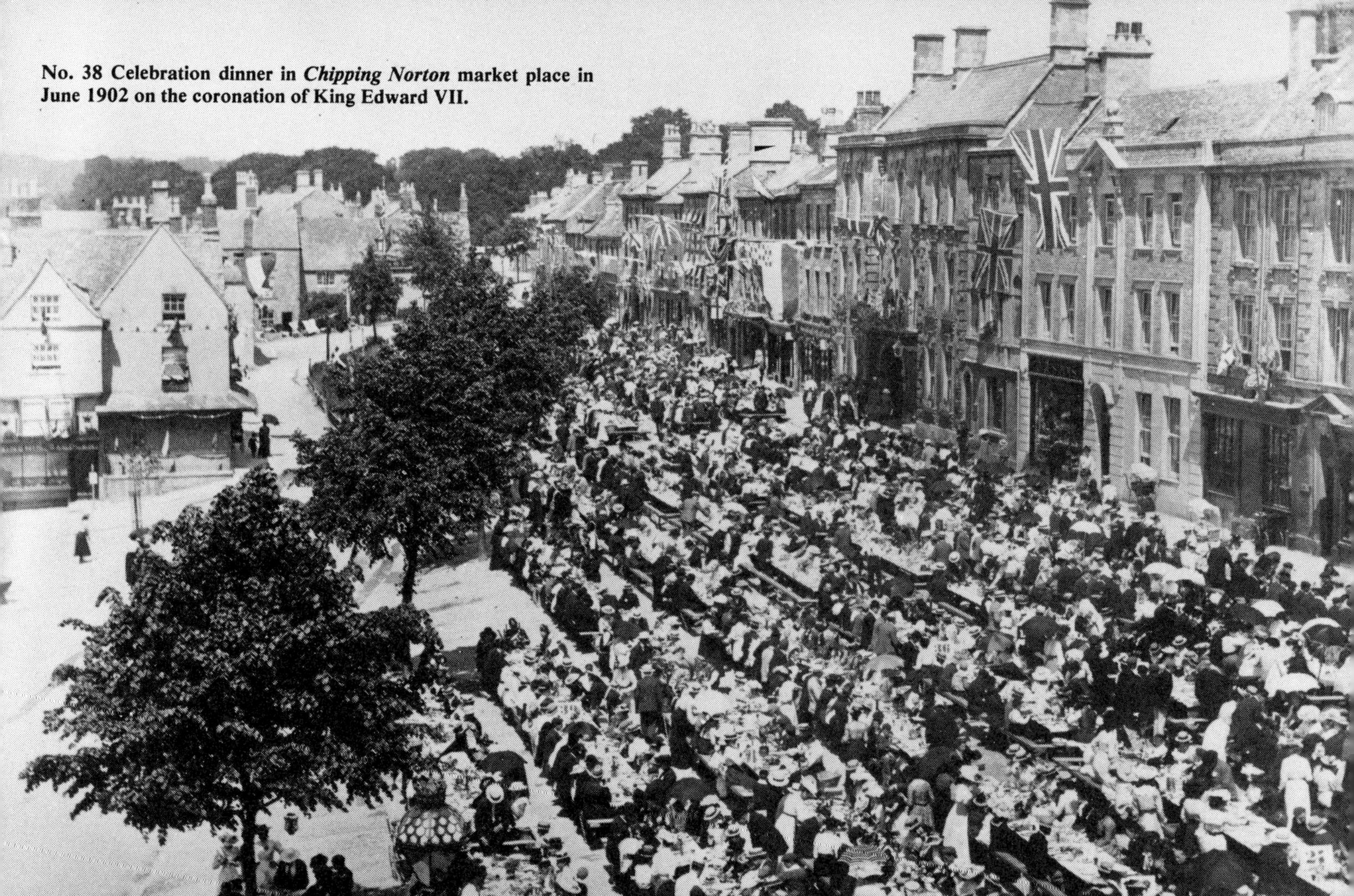

No. 38 Celebration dinner in *Chipping Norton* market place in June 1902 on the coronation of King Edward VII.

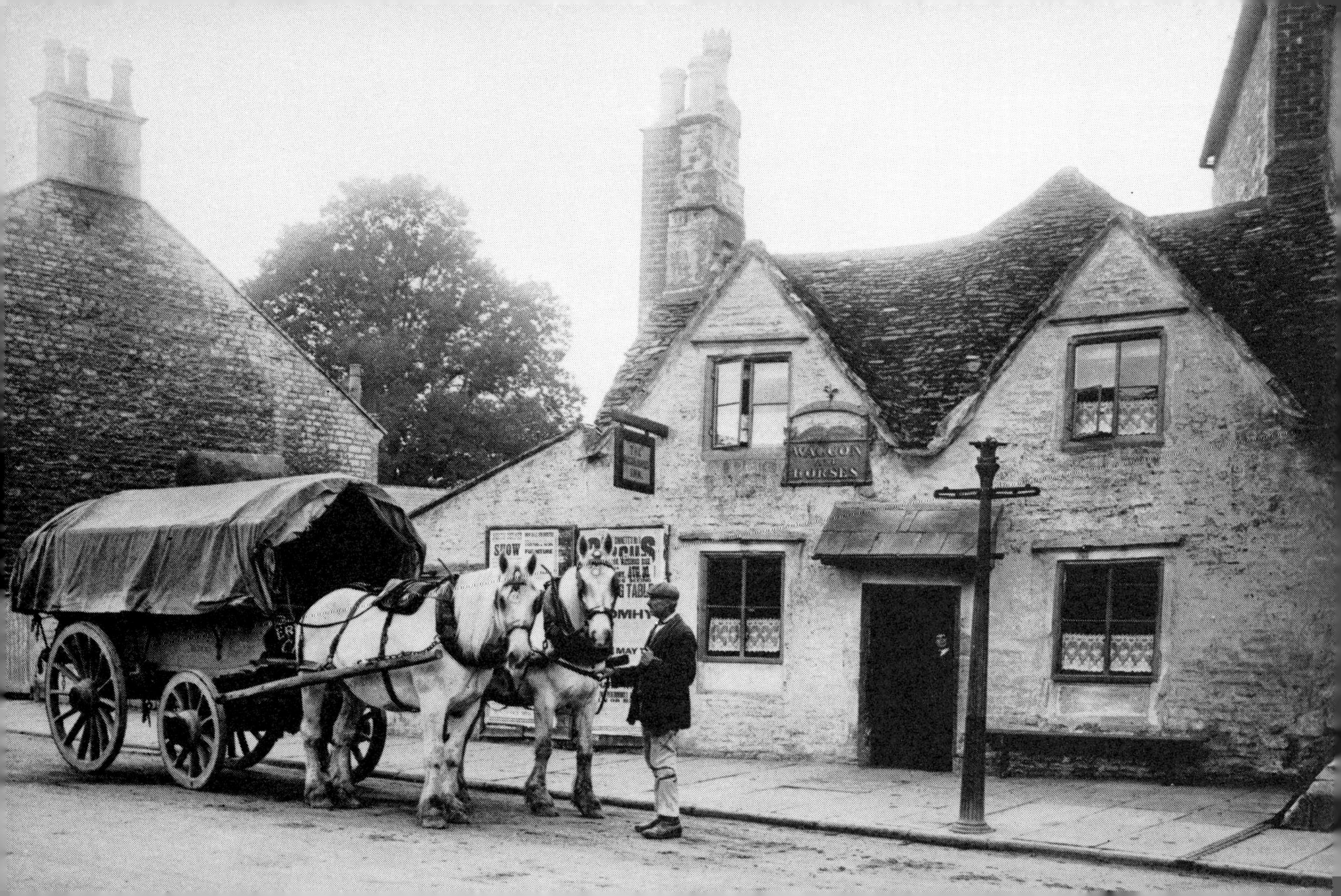
WAGGON
HORSES
SHOW

TRANSPORT

No. 39 (left) Transport by road remained difficult and slow until well into the present century. The carrier was the only form of regular communication until bus services began, and farm workers relied upon their own transport for moving goods to and from the market town. On one such journey returning home from *Cirencester,* a pause outside the Waggon & Horses Inn gives the photographer ample opportunity to achieve an association of ideas with the name of the inn.

No. 40 (overleaf) Public transport for the fortunate few in this four in hand outside the Bull Hotel in *Fairford* market place early this century. Has this photograph been deliberately posed?

No. 41 (overleaf) Outside the same hotel, the first motor bus service in the area was introduced between Cirencester and Lechlade in 1904. Its popularity (and curiosity value) is obvious.

Nos. 42 & 43 (overleaf) Apart from the Swindon to Gloucester via Stroud line of the Great Western Railway (1841–5) and the Oxford, Worcester & Wolverhampton Railway (opened 1853), the railway routes across the Cotswolds tended to be late additions to the national network and largely insignificant in other than local traffic.
Perhaps the most interesting was the last built, the Midland & South Western Junction Railway originally projected as part of a grand scheme to link Manchester with Southampton by rail.
These two remarkable photographs – only recently identified – show the construction work in progress at *Chedworth* in 1888. No. 42 shows the northern approach to Chedworth tunnel where 480 navvies, 630 horses, 5 locos and one steam excavator were employed night and day through the summer, the men living in temporary accommodation alongside the workings.
No. 43 is one of the contractor's locomotives suitably named in the traditional manner for Cirencester. The railway was opened in 1891 but struggled constantly for survival and was absorbed by its arch rival the G.W.R. in 1923. It was closed to passengers in 1961.

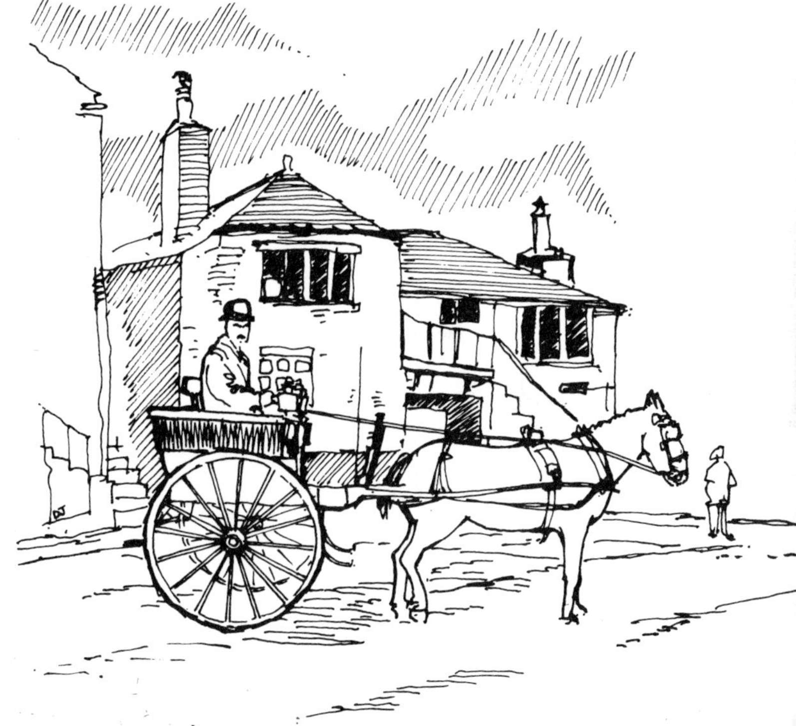

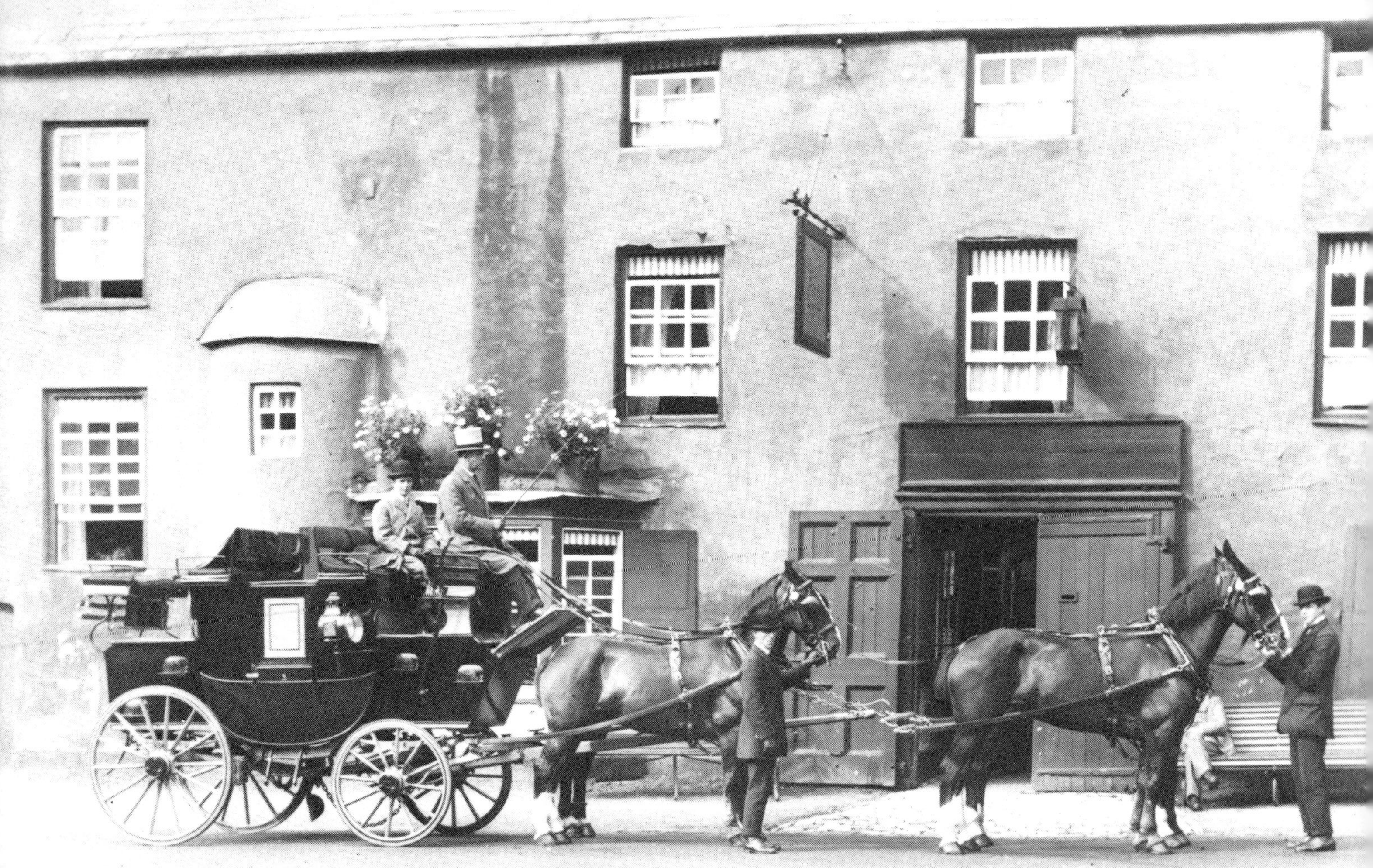

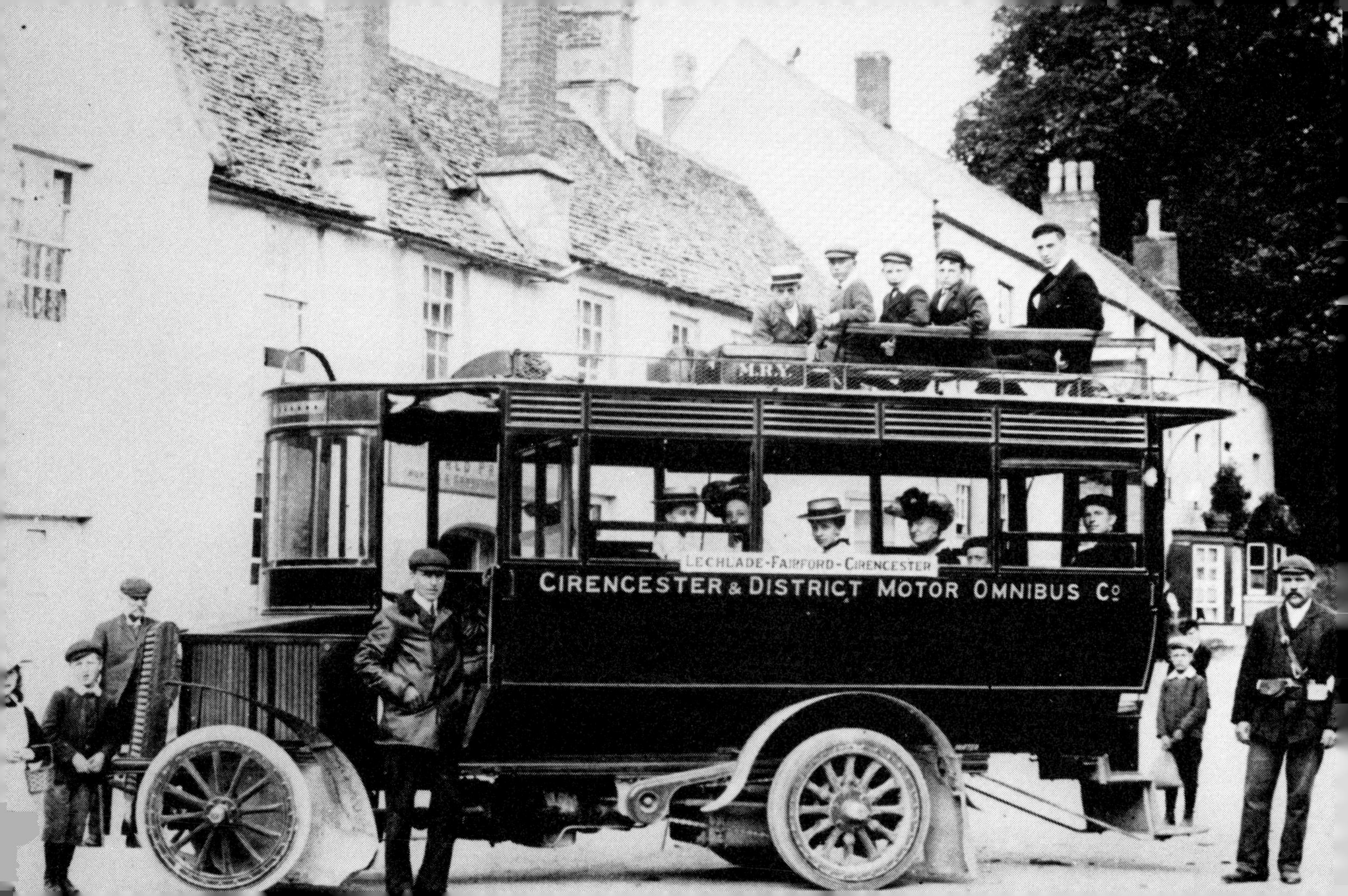
M.R.Y.
LECHLADE-FAIRFORD-CIRENCESTER
CIRENCESTER & DISTRICT MOTOR OMNIBUS Co

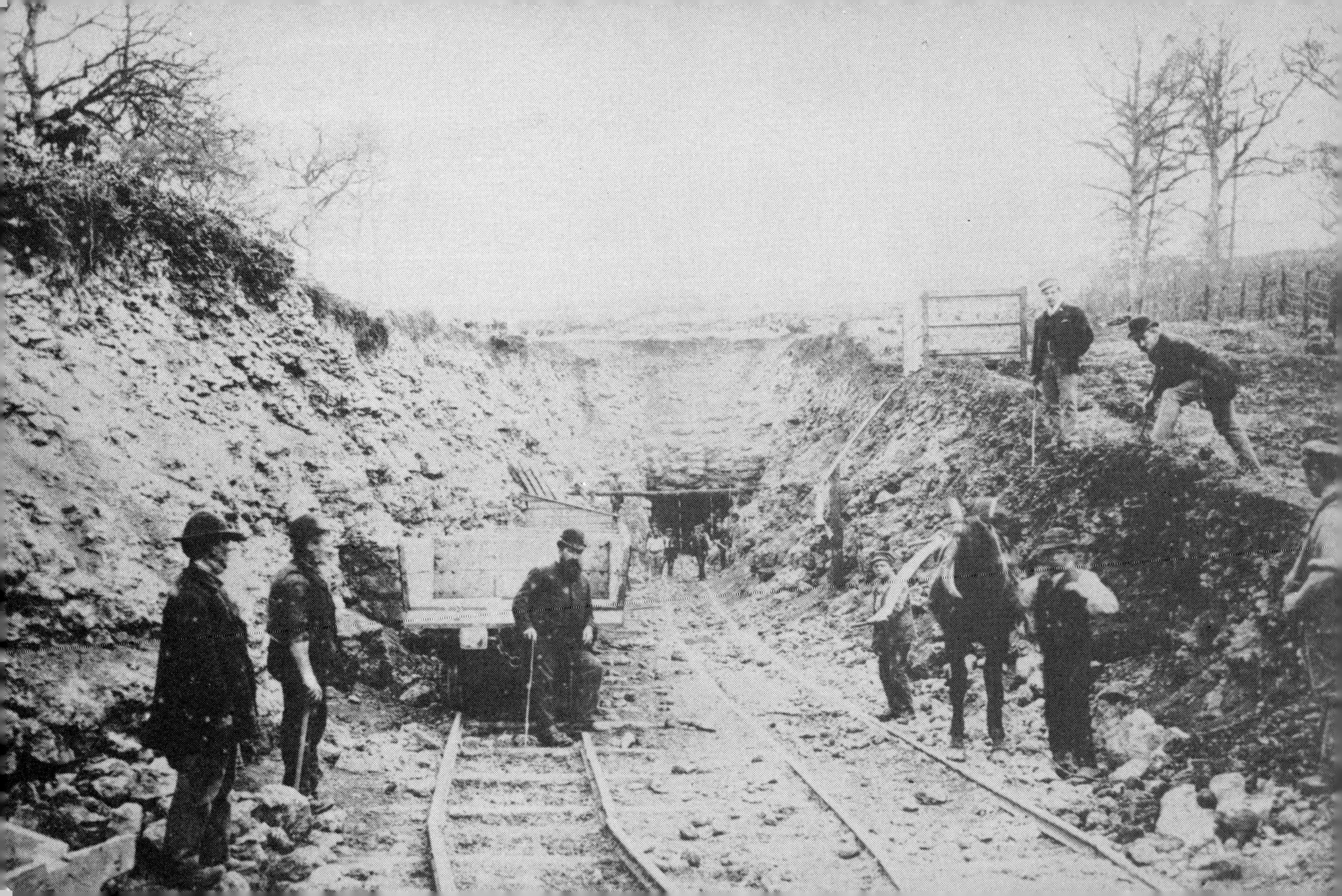

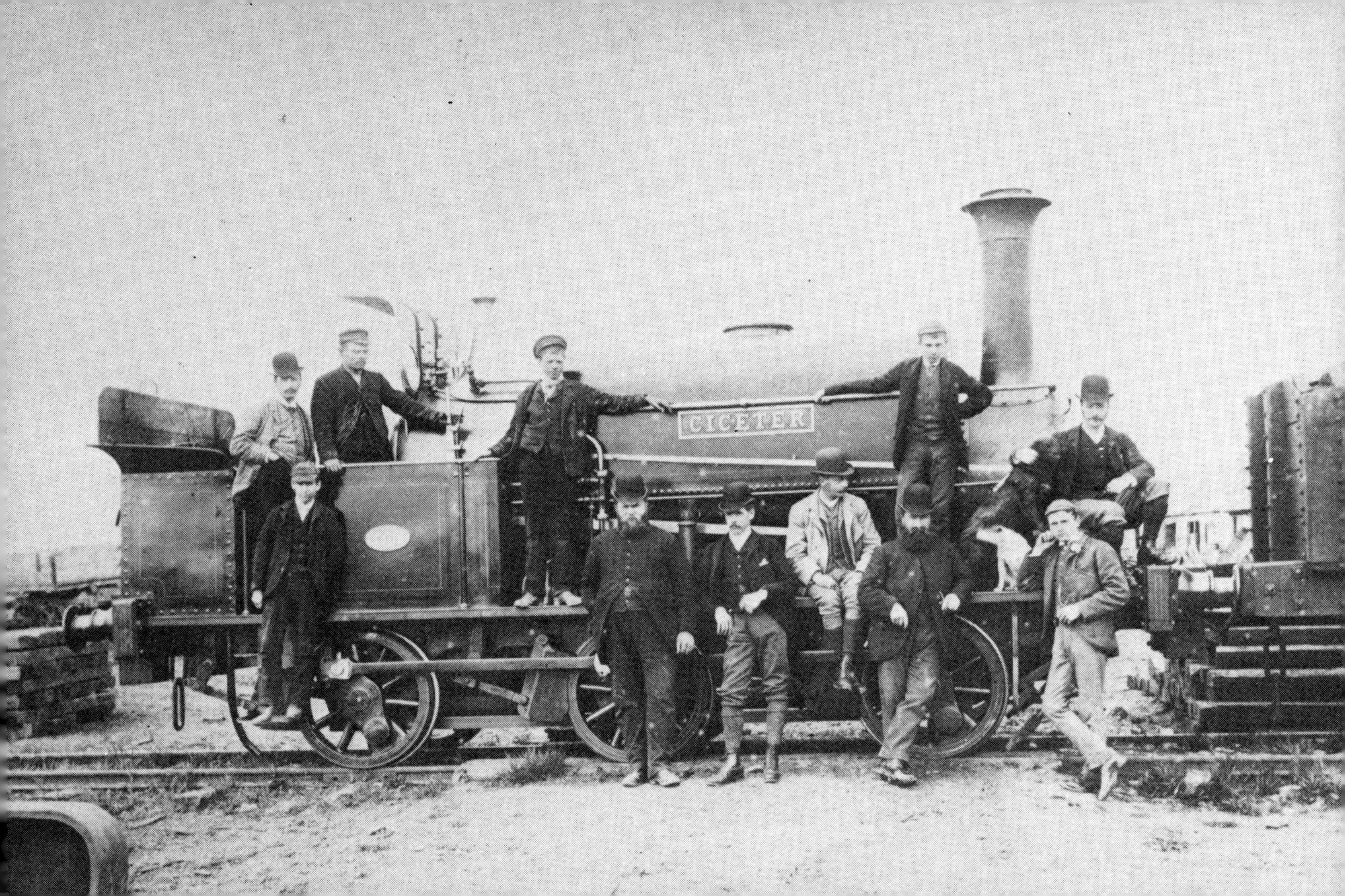
CICETER

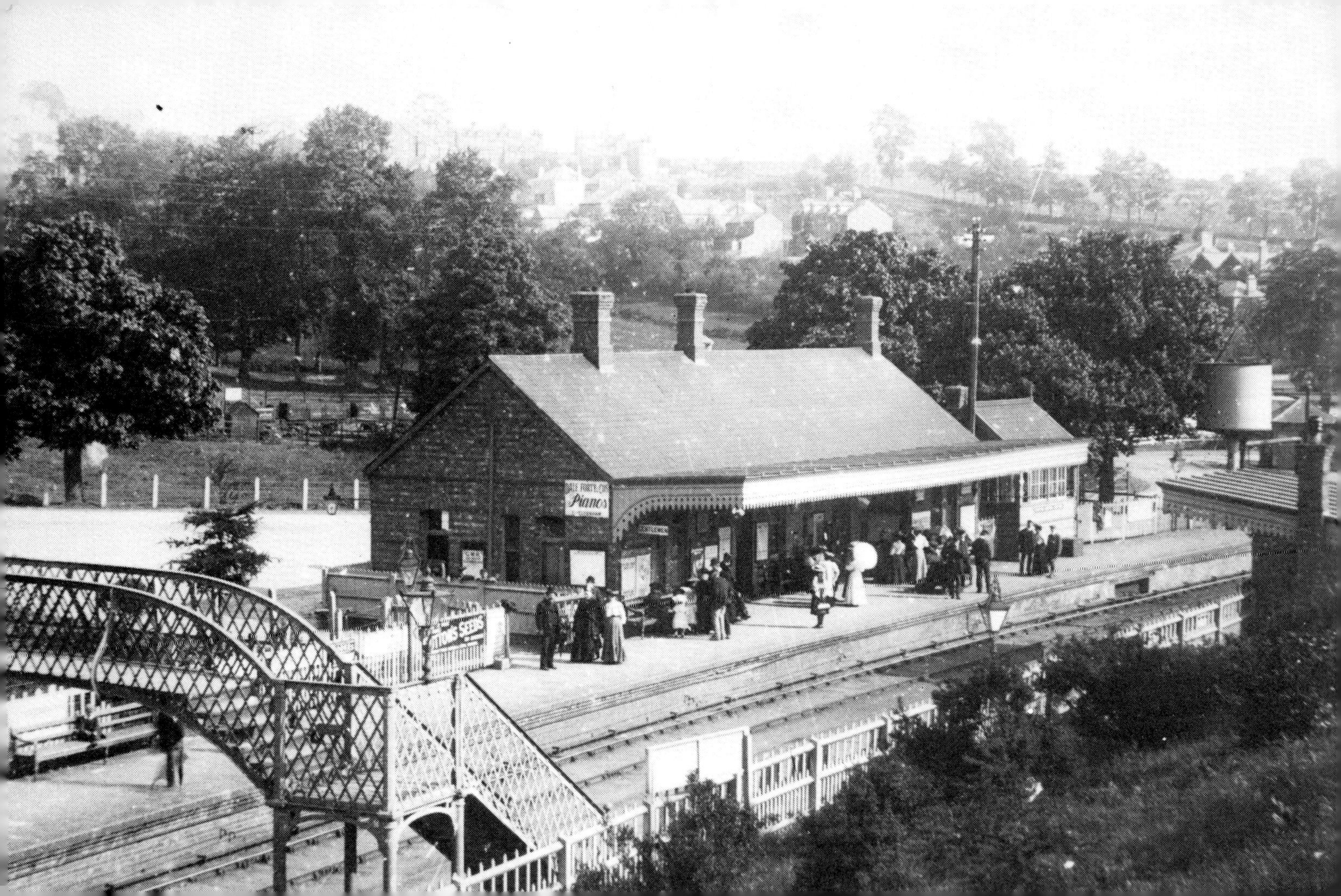

Pianos
SEEDS